Readers have loved
NO HOLY COWS IN BUSINESS

Principles of entrepreneurship that can help change the way you do business. A recommended read.

- Afternoon Despatch & Courier

I salute your effort. The title & the cover are great. I think it's a book that one should gift to young budding entrepreneurs before they set out.

- Amitava Datta, start-up & team building specialist, also a 'struggling entrepreneur'

A perfect guide book of the Do's and Don'ts to be followed while running a business and building it.

- APN News

An excellent read and answers questions as to why I am an entrepreneur-consultant which I have never bothered to ask.

- Mohan Sundar Rajan, CEO, Paradigm Shift PR

Kiran and Sekhar... have spent enough time in the laboratories of entrepreneurship to understand the ground rules and communicate them to the entrepreneur of today.

- Business for all

I wish this book had been available two decades ago when I began my career.

- Manish Kulkarni, chief co-ordinator, BDB Book Club

A wonderful addition to the libraries of educational institutes. A must read for start-ups and also for those in the early stages of their entrepreneurial journey.

- Business India

A remarkable book which every budding entrepreneur should read... highlights how to negotiate the dangerous hair-pin bends, speed breakers and slippery tracks on the road to entrepreneurship.

- Chandran Iyer, Founder Editor, Corporate Tycoons

Its USPs – putting forth a standpoint, and illustrating it with live examples of successful people. Slices of biography, genesis of well-known businesses, anecdotes, human touches, all real-life lore, make it all the more invaluable.

- Corporate Citizen

Not only offers good insights into the world of entrepreneurship through case-studies and interviews but also provides a bird's eye view through nine guiding principles.

- Corporate Tycoons

The book is clearly written and in simple English. Reminds me of R.K. Narayanan's style. Not wasting any one's time by repeating concepts over and over again.

- Dr Lakshman Mahadevan, Assistant Professor,
Emporia State University, Kansas

Chipping at the solid block of entrepreneurship to discover what lies inside, the book works on two levels – while it outlines nine fundamental principles to guide green-horn entrepreneurs to tread the right path and not indulge in mistakes that can cost them dear, it also intersperses these with interviews of leading industrialists and businessmen.

- Industrial Products Finder

This book gives clear insight of how great business people think about the future and their company. Great work. Keep it up.

- Krishna Lakamsani, CEO,
IPay Tech India Pvt. Ltd, Lakamsani Group

Unique examples from all over the country. Unknown people, who have struggled and yet never given up but made a success of their projects. Many interesting and motivating examples... great learning, that nothing comes easy.

- Lila F. Poonawalla, Chairperson. Lila Poonawalla Foundation

The fact that an advertising professional and a business scribe have been able to sell the first edition of their book in four months, is a testimony that within every journalist also lies an entrepreneur and vice-versa.

- Sakal Times

An intro to career focus areas for young people and as reminders for senior folks... very coherently and compellingly developed.

- Shyamal Sen, Partner and Global Lead
-Financial Services Solutions and Technologies,
Computer Sciences Corporation, New York

Deals with business, success and failure; business as a medium to contribute to society and other related issues.

- TGS

Very lucid, makes comprehension easy due to the live examples. Cause and effect methodology so as to understand the decision making required.

- Dr. R. Krishna, Director - Corporate Relations,
Universal Business School, Karjat

May the entire business world of India avail itself of the principles Sekhar and Kiran have so brilliantly exposed, so that the book will run into multiple editions!.

- Fr G.K. Carlson, sj, Kew, Australia

NO HOLY COWS
IN BUSINESS...

9 Principles of Entrepreneurship

———— ❧ ————

Kiran Bhat and Sekhar Seshan
www.noholycows.com

VISHWAKARMA
PUBLICATIONS
VP

NO HOLY COWS IN BUSINESS...

1st Edition - Aug. 2014
Reprint - Feb. 2015
© Kiran Bhat & Sekhar Seshan

ISBN 978-93-83572-20-5

Published by:
Vishwakarma Publications
283, Budhwar Peth, Near City Post,
Pune- 411 002.
Phone No: 020 24448989 / 20261157
Email: info@vpindia.co.in
Website: www.vpindia.co.in

Cover Design Credits
Pallavi Desai,
Art Director, Xebec Communications

Typeset and Layout
Goldfish Graphics, Pune.

Printed by
Repro India Limited, Mumbai.

I wish I had read this book when I started off my entrepreneurial journey in 1996, at the age of 21. This is a must-read for all those who get bitten by the entrepreneurial bug. There is a unique Indian context to it which most globally successful books don't provide. The hard truths around customers and dealing with them when the rubber meets the road especially resonated with me.

- Narayan Rajan,
Founder CEO, i-Vista Digital Solutions Pvt Ltd, Bangalore

This is an extremely readable and practical book for all practitioners and aspirants in the world of Indian business. Practical tips on leadership, well articulated and embellished with local cases and interviews make this a great addition to the book list of all entrepreneurs academicians and corporate participants.

- Dr Ganesh Natarajan,
Vice Chairman and Global CEO, Zensar Technologies

Entrepreneurship has never been easy in India. But the times are changing, which means literature on the subject is not just good reading but also vital for the new generation of risk takers. No Holy Cows is a tapestry of the experiences of Indian entrepreneurs who have succeeded against the odds (and some who have failed too). With the new emphasis on entrepreneurship at Indian B-schools, this book is a must for every MBA library.

- Parthasarathi Swami,
Managing Editor, Asia Region, Knowledge@Wharton

The book describes in a simple way the pre-requisites needed to become a successful entrepreneur. What I liked in particular is the way in which the key points have been put forward and then elaborated and substantiated with real case stories of recent times. Most of the case stories would be inspiring for the upcoming entrepreneurs. The book is a good reminder and a guide for a few Do's and Don'ts in our business life. I wish great success to the publication, especially for the benefit of upcoming young entrepreneurs. There are lots of them in India who want to be successful.

- Subodh S.Nadkarni, President - Europe, Russia, Middle East, Africa, Asia, Sulzer Rotating Equipment Services, Switzerland

The first and last principles are really thought-provoking. Loving what you are doing is really crucial to running a start-up, but this is never enunciated – maybe it's taken for granted. And I really appreciate the advice to "pull the plug when it does not make any sense". Many entrepreneurs face major issues, but keep on spending – it's like being hooked on races, where you keep putting money on horses and losing it. Adding new revenue streams is a bit of a paradox: it can reduce your focus on the main business; but it's good if done judiciously. The case study approach makes the book more practical, with real people coming to life in real-life Indian situations which all entrepreneurs here can understand and identify with.

- Pramod M. Chaudhari,
Executive Chairman, Praj Industries Ltd, Pune

Acknowledgements

I would like to dedicate this book to my mom who inspired me to become something in life and to my dad who gave me wings to fly. I would also like to thank all my clients who taught me how to run a business and my very hardworking team who support me in all my endeavours.

Above all I would like to express my deepest gratitude to Him without whom I would not have been able to write a single word. Last but not the least, I would like to thank my co-author Sekhar who travelled the length and breadth of the country meeting people and writing their stories.

-Kiran Bhat

My thanks go first to Ashok H. Advani, writing for whom in Business India magazine for a quarter of a century got me across the threshold of many doors that would otherwise have been closed to me. This also taught me real-life lessons some of which I have quoted from in the book. Thanks also to all the friends, business honchos and entrepreneurs who helped me with interviews, prompt responses to my e-mails and quick 'previews' to quote on the back cover. My wife Radhika and daughters Nisha and Varsha have been unfailingly supportive of all my work. And thanks, Kiran, for giving me the opportunity – let's do it again!

- Sekhar Seshan

Prologue

Why do some people do well in business and others fail miserably? Even after a debacle, some bounce back very quickly and others never really recover. Business, obviously, is not for everybody.

Why not? Why can't more people become entrepreneurs?

Business fuels the economy and creates jobs. That seems simple enough. But why do certain communities excel through generations, giving them an edge in business, while others are not drawn to entrepreneurship? While such questions arise in everyone's mind at some point, the good news is that there is no real qualification to succeed in business. Why, you don't even need a degree!

When we say 'business' in this book, we are addressing the first-generation entrepreneur. A business which has been around for a couple of generations would have laid down its own ground rules and evolved some kind of a formula for success. Business is a natural self-expression for some communities. They are so aligned with it that for them it is not work. They, in fact, may not even distinguish between work and play. Their life and family revolves around the business and every family member is enrolled in it.

Kirana stores are prime examples of this. You will see the husband manning the counter, the sons and assorted nephews doing door delivery and the women and girls sorting out the grains and dals to create their own, albeit unbranded, private labels.

So what can you term as a business?

A business is an organisation or enterprising entity engaged in commercial, industrial or professional activities (source: Google)

Loosely, a business consists of the following:

- There is a product/service for customers.

- Customers: those who consume the product or service; add, serve, keep them for life as long as they are profitable.

- Team: people who serve the customer.

- Revenue: profit and loss which is generated by the business.

- Cash flow: the cash the business generates or loses

- Goodwill: created by the business because of satisfied customers.

- Capital: the seed money deployed in the business

This is all really the essence of what an entrepreneur in a business handles.

So, who is an entrepreneur? A person who operates a business / businesses taking on financial risks, he or she is a person who manages a business undertaking assuming the risk for the sake of profit.

Is there a difference between an entrepreneur and somebody who just runs a business? Once you read all the chapters, you can make that judgement yourself.

But what really constitutes success in a business? Is there a formula after all? I am a first-generation entrepreneur and after many years with several ups and downs, have lived to tell the tale.

I have tried to encapsulate the basic tenets of entrepreneurship into 9 primary principles.

I started my business career 22 years ago. I would never have thought back then, that I would work for a large corporation, start three companies and an angel investment fund, become a business author, a motivational speaker and consultant, and go out of business more than once. It has been a crazy ride, but with age, and all those ups and downs, comes experience—and with experience comes a little bit of wisdom. Here are 9 lessons I wish I had learned before I was 40.

When I decided to write this book to help would-be entrepreneurs, I asked Sekhar Seshan, eminent business journalist and old friend, to help me with meeting and interviewing entrepreneurs across the length and breadth of the country. Sekhar does this best. In his career spanning four decades, he has met thousands of entrepreneurs about whom he has written in Business India- and later in other business magazines. Their experiences, as ably recounted by him in this book, have proved to be invaluable.

I am very grateful to Dr. S.B. Mujumdar who very gracefully accepted to write the foreword for this book. Being an entrepreneur and a doyen of management education in India he is truly inspiring. He wrote it in record time despite his very hectic schedule.

Disclaimer: Although there are 9 principles as a guideline to entrepreneurship, in reality there are no holy cows because anybody can become an entrepreneur. You don't really need any special qualification for it.

All you do need is enthusiasm, passion, ability to learn continuously, perseverance and an ability to get up and dust yourself quickly after every fall as fall you will periodically.

So it is not that your Dad / family has to be in business before you take the plunge. Or even that you need to have access to huge capital or connections.

All you need is the guts to take the plunge.

Kiran Bhat

Foreword

Padma Bhushan Dr. S.B. Mujumdar
Chancellor, Symbiosis International University

'Why can't more people become entrepreneurs?'

This is the question Kiran Bhat and Sekhar Sesan ask in their book 'NO HOLY COWS IN BUSINESS'. This question is asked by many. Innumerable books, many seminars and workshops are arranged. Management Gurus earn lakhs of rupees by charging heavy fees from those eager to become entrepreneurs. But how many of them turn out to be successful entrepreneurs? Can you become an entrepreneur by reading books or attending seminars? The answer is 'YES' and 'NO'. It depends on how serious and sincere you are.

Kiran in her own inimitable style tries to motivate her readers and navigates them towards entrepreneurship with the help of her co-author, Sekhar Seshan. Throughout the book they cite examples of ordinary people becoming extraordinary and those who made the impossible possible. My congratulations to Kiran and Sekhar on giving live examples of entrepreneurship not from the U.S.A. or the

U.K., France or Germany but those from our own Bharat and India.

Take for example the case study of T. Naryan Shanbhag, who started Strand Book Stall. He was the first bookseller awarded a Padma Shri by the President of India. He started the book stall in an empty corner of a cinema house. With tremendous perseverance and patience he made it into a reputed bookstore of India. His patrons ranged from Pandit Nehru to Shri Yashwantrao Chavan.

In order to achieve success in life what one needs is innovation, passion – that fire in the belly – and even compassion. You need to change and adapt to it quickly. N.R. Narayanamurthy goes further. He says, 'At every stage of Infosys I changed first.'

Readers of the book will find several such case studies of Indians and that is what makes it not only readable but a practical guide to become an entrepreneur.

You should strive to be an entrepreneur because it empowers you to make money by starting a business even when this involves taking financial risk. You don't learn swimming by reading books on it. You have to be trained and, more importantly, you need to jump into the water. This first jump is the risk without which you can't swim. Taking a risk is the first step towards becoming an entrepreneur.

This book will help the first-generation entrepreneurs who have to struggle with many aspects of business of which he (or she) may not be aware. They will not have a family background or experience to guide them. The principles enunciated here can come in handy. The book will also help management students who want to start their own business.

Contents

Principle 1   01
Love what you are doing
Interview: Harshvardhan Neotia, Chairman,
Ambuja Neotia Group, Kolkata
Case Study: Heady with Wine

Principle 2   18
An organization is the reflection of the promoter's energy
Interview: Chandra Mohan, Padmashri,
Founder Chairman, Punjab Tractors Ltd (PTL)
Case Study: Booked!

Principle 3   36
Focus, focus, focus
Interview: C. Parthasarathy, Chairman, Karvy Group
Case Study: Will-power, tolerance and perseverance

Principle 4   52
Get financial literacy
Interview: Dr Anil Lamba, Founder & Director,
Lamcom School of Management
Case Study: Lessons of Liberalisation

Principle 5   75
Add a new revenue stream every year
Start an incubation and then scale it up.
Interview: Vikram S. Kirloskar, vice chairman,
Toyota Kirloskar Motor
Case Study 1: Sticking to the knitting
Case Study 2: Forward integration - and stepping sideways

Principle 6   93
Keep costs under control at all times.
Not only during recession.
Interview: G.V. Krishna Reddy, Chairman, GVK Group
Case Study 1: Sticking to the knitting
Case Study 2: Forward integration - and stepping sideways

Principle 7   109
Enrolment of key people for the next level
Interview: Suhas Baxi, CEO, Pennar Industries Ltd
Case Study: Advantages become disadvantages

Principle 8   128
Continuous learning
Interview: Nishit Kumar, Founder MD, NOTRE Group
Case Study 1: How a very key learning intervention
can change lives?.
Case Study 2: Using a learning approach, late in life,
to improve your own efficiency
Case study 3: A corollary to lifelong learning
is learning about oneself

Principle 9   143
Pull the plug when it does not make any sense
Interview: T. Muralidharan, Founder & Chairman,
TMI Group
Case Study: No lobsters in the pot!

Epilogue   153

About the Authors   157

Appendix / Acronyms   159

Index   161

Love what you are doing

You must have read this ad nauseam in every management book. But I have a different perspective. It is compulsory to love what you are doing. At this juncture you think this is going into the realm of rigmarole. But hang in there. When you love and enjoy what you are doing, you do not mind doing it year after year for the rest of your life or for as long as you are in business. The quote 'business is like riding a bicycle — while you keep pedalling you won't fall off' is really true.

The amazing thing about this principle is, it is a continuous game. You can never relax, put your feet up and say, that's it... I am done for the year and have reached my target. The best is always yet to come. It is all about continuously adding value to your business, continuous innovation, cost control, improving processes which will in turn improve quality, deliver better customer satisfaction, better product quality, better service, better HR practices, employee satisfaction, training... phew, the list just goes on.

An entrepreneur has to continuously measure qualitative aspects of the business along with the quantitative. There is real merit in the latter. In my own case, being in the creative business we never paid attention to quantity for a number of years. But if we as businesses want to scale up, this is absolutely necessary. Scaling up is all about quantifying results, measurement metrics, tools and of course people who can handle scale.

Now, if you truly do not like what you are doing, how long will you survive? The learning and lessons are relentless. Success is rare and the world of business is strewn with failures. Most of you know that famous statistic: only 5 percent of businesses actually survive. Perhaps just 1 percent thrive.

I myself went bust at least twice. The first time we had two large client defaults. I was naive and wet behind the ears. After my initial success, when we had blue-chip clients who did not pose any problem of credit risk, we went on to handling clients who definitely were not creditworthy. At that point I did not know how to distinguish between a creditworthy client and a non-creditworthy one. Just because one client was good for ₹10 crore another might not even be good for ₹50 lakh. Back then, I was unable to distinguish between the two.

Trust me, it sounds very elementary when I write it, but I can bet my last rupee that there will be thousands of entrepreneurs out there who are not aware of this simple fact. This is simply not taught to us in school and college. We have to learn these lessons through the hard knocks of life. We had an issue of huge outstanding dues with this client. We had to go for litigation and guess what? We won the case after 8-9 years — but the money is still at large.

Lesson learnt — if a person does not have the intention to pay, even if he is your next door neighbour you can do nothing about it. Also in India people who default will be happy if you go to court as they are fully aware of the time it takes for any case to reach its conclusion.

As Sulajja Firodia Motwani, who ran Kinetic Honda, said when she took over 20th Century Finance: "Our agents in the field are all local people who know every potential borrower's intention to pay. That is a much more important yardstick than the ability to pay!"

The second time, we had a client whose billing ran into crores. One of our branch offices did not follow basic processes and systems and did not do time-to-time reconciliation. This ended very badly for us where we had to write off a substantial amount..

Now you may ask, what has all this got to do with loving what you are doing?

Well, first of all mistakes made by anybody in the team ultimately lands on your table for a clean-up. So you had better be aware of everything that is happening. The credit is all for the team but debit is all for you. Be prepared for that. You need to have the ability to write off amounts and go through really hard times and motivate yourself enough to bounce back. Now if you do not love what you are doing do you think you will be able to withstand all this?

So check whether you are cut out to be an entrepreneur.

Questions to ask yourself:

When all else is closing in on me, do I have the guts and ability to carry on? Can I quickly move from bust to boom pretty much seamlessly? Can I pick myself up quickly, dust away the debris and move on after one failure?

Can I motivate myself regularly (there will be no boss to do it for you) and with very little family support?

Can I be a student for life?

Do I have the wherewithal for continuous creation? So only if the business is your natural self-expression, can you thrive and do well. Then you can bounce back from setbacks. Life will be play, not work. Also, remember — less than 1 percent of the world's population are meant to be entrepreneurs with the ability to do all this. Nothing is stopping the other 99 percent — but trust me, it is not easy. Most of us expect life to be one long picnic where even if the maid, milkman or driver does not turn up for work we treat it as a major catastrophe. Running a business is not meant for everybody — especially managing people, finances, clients/customers, training, resource allocation, purchase — in short, the works.

Tip: Meditation or quiet time every day helps enormously.

Passion for their businesses is what has driven the following people to achieve important milestones.

"More than just 'fire in the belly', you must be like a mad dog – fight, fight, fight!" says A.D. Padmasingh Isaac, founder CMD of the Chennai-based Aachi masala. "An entrepreneur should dream during the daytime — and at night, he should not sleep but keep his imagination working." The 57-year-old, who set up his own business only when he was 43, is of the firm belief that nobody can promote a product better than the producer himself.

A.D. Padmasingh Isaac, founder CMD, Aachi masala, Chennai

He prefers to do things himself, rather than hiring 'expert' market research and other consultants. Every morning, when he goes for a walk, he makes it a point to look into at least 10 dustbins on his route. "I check what brands of spices and masalas the people living in the neighbourhood use," he explains. "If I find a lot of empty Aachi packets, I am happy. But when I see other brands, I make a note – and when I reach office I ask my R&D team to buy those and analyse them to find out what they have that ours doesn't!" When he created a Kozhambu (a kind of sambar) masala to differentiate his brand, he went to the market and hawked it himself, because the existing shopkeepers refused to risk keeping an untested product. Today, it is a ₹100-crore product in his 160-product basket of ₹560 crore. Isaac still heads his marketing team, and knows every member of his sales force personally.

Y. Rajeev Reddy, CMD,
Country Club, Hyderabad

Passion rules the life of Y. Rajeev Reddy, the man with a smile under a bushy moustache who is always making a thumbs-up sign out at you from hoardings and newspaper advertisements. "I'm really not a businessman," insists the CMD of Country Club in Hyderabad. "I'm marketing a concept." Rajeev Reddy's life revolves round his 'baby' as he nurtures its growth, takes it places – all over India, to Dubai… even Africa, London and New York – to give his members a good time. He set up his first club in the centre of Hyderabad in 1995, and "could have stayed with just that and been happy, like many others" – but he wanted to give the company a pan-Indian and global presence. "I overcame many challenges, starting with prohibition in Andhra Pradesh in 1995," he says. "Membership dropped drastically – maybe that was what pushed us to expand!"

And expand he did: Country Club India is now a multi—million dollar entity, with 55 own properties, 175 franchised establishments, over a staggering 4000 affiliations across the world and recognition by the Limca Book of World Records as the country's biggest chain of family clubs. "This is an enthusiasm business!" its founder grins. That's something he proved personally, when he went on a strict diet to lose weight for a sky-diving stunt he performed to launch his Dubai property.

Achal Bakeri, CMD of the ₹1,100-crore Symphony Ltd, was a youth with fire in his belly, too. The son of a civil engineer who

Achal Bakeri, CMD,
Symphony Ltd, Ahmedabad

had established a real estate development company in Ahmedabad, he accompanied his father on site visits during his holidays. "Even as a child, I found buildings very fascinating – I used to draw building plans when I was six or seven years old," he says.

The young Achal's goal was to get into the family business, so he studied architecture at the Centre for Environment, Planning, and Technology in Ahmedabad, then real estate finance at the University of Southern California's Marshall School of Business. Back home, he realized that he no longer wanted to join the family business and "be a cog in the wheel". So what was he to do? He had just moved house, and installed air coolers because air-conditioners were not possible in a number of areas of the new place. "What was available was of horrible quality. My father suggested, why not design a good one?" The idea struck a chord, and Symphony was born. He stuck with his venture through disaster – when an ill-advised expansion into other products eroded the company's entire net worth and made it a BIFR basket case – and built it up to the world's largest air cooler manufacturer, selling over half a million units a year in 60-plus countries.

In Gurgaon, Jayant Davar came out of engineering college armed with a degree and the typical entrepreneur's passion, and did not accept an MBA scholarship he won. His father D.N. Davar, a banker of 45 years' experience and former chairman of the Industrial Finance Corporation of India, had seen many start-ups becoming wind-ups and advised the young Jayant against going into business. "But my son was very adamant, so I had to support him," says the senior Davar – who financed the setting up of what is now the ₹1,600-crore, 7,000-people Sandhar Technologies Ltd., and even became the company Chairman. Remembers Jayant, the company's vice chairman and MD: "He had kept aside some ₹ 30,000 or ₹ 35,000 for my sister's marriage, but he gave it to me as seed capital. He put up the money for a belief system with which he didn't agree." With that – then grudging – encouragement, Jayant could follow his dream and passion. "I believe very strongly that you have no reason not to give your best if you start something you are passionate about," says the man who believes that picking up anything as a challenge gives you better gratification, and that if you really push the limits, you get success. And so, he keeps taking on new businesses which have nothing to do with the others: from car locks to mirrors, door handles to aluminium castings – for which he has acquired a company in Spain – and a wheel manufacturing unit and one that makes plastics for the back panels of television sets: one totally new business every few years. "My case study is now taught in 17 business schools around the world!' says the man who decided against doing an MBA himself.

The most important and critical question you need to ask yourself is, why am I in business?

Remember that you are also an employee. The bigger purpose why you are in business is to create a product or service which serves a customer, creates jobs, fuels or is part of that ecosystem. So you are only a custodian of the business and do not really own anything. Knowing this, you can sleep peacefully at night. If you have got into this field for the right reasons, then the next paragraph is not for you. What if you have got into it for the wrong reasons?

So what are these wrong reasons? There is really only one: a really big one.

Wrong reason No 1: To become rich.

You will surely stop reading this book right here. Why on earth will I want to get into business if not to become rich is what you are already thinking, right? Sure, wealth is certainly one of the reasons. But the primary reason and really the only reason you are in business is to solve a problem.

Whose problem? Your client's problem. Your customer's problem. Only if a client has a problem or something which needs a solution will he come to you. Why else? If things were going swimmingly well he would not need you.

So the real reason you are an Entrepreneur is to solve a problem, and give a solution. The solution could be as simple as delivering bread and milk in the morning to providing auto ancillaries for clients.

Let's examine some of the solutions you can provide:

1. **Kirana store:** What is it really doing? It offers door delivery. It is not the sugar, milk you are really buying. You are buying the quick, any-time delivery service. So as for the MNCs there, can a large-format store really give you quick door delivery? That too for a value of not more than ₹ 50, and sometimes even less? A customer may order only 1/2 ltr of milk and ask the store owner to throw in some biscuits just to increase value.

2. **Florist:** What is the challenge? You are providing an idea and a delivery to a loved one or to a business associate. You may be far away and may have even forgotten a birthday. So the additional service is reminding you about D-Day and delivery.

3. **Auto ancillary:** The automobile companies today want to increase profitability in an era of spiralling cost and squeezed margins. They want a vendor who can invest and give spare parts just in time. Quality and design are hygiene factors which may not necessarily be paid for. So what is the real service? Finance, isn't it?

4. **Advertising agency:** The media part of the business is really — and only — finance. The creative part of the business is to help a client move his product or service at a faster pace than last year. It is also to help him build a brand and create/maintain the premium of the said product and service.

5. **Automobile companies:** What is the problem they are solving in this time and age? Surely not transportation! The problem they are solving is that they are helping you manage/maintain/enhance your image in society. A luxury car solves a basic challenge. It communicates that you have arrived, when you are doing well enough to keep buying new models of luxury sedans/SUVs. It also solves an underlying need of enhancing your worth in your own eyes. The more a product/service can enhance your own worth the higher the premium that can be charged. This is true for luxury cars, hand bags, shoes, jewellery, etc.

You can make your own list of the real services you are providing.

So what have we really done here? I have provided different contexts for you to view the service you are providing. The business you are in, or its nomenclature is for the society or for your client. It is not for you to identify yourself with. However, you know the real context and value of your business.

So if you feel you cannot love providing the service you are currently providing you are free to switch to the service you would really like to provide.

Recently we stayed at a tiger resort. Why did we choose this resort over the others?

Pench Tiger Resort: Sandeep Singh loves what he is doing. He loves wildlife, is a conservationist, takes his guests personally on safaris, is very knowledgeable about the flora and fauna and about the forest itself. So is it any wonder that people coming to Pench will choose to stay with Sandeep Singh? Why would they not choose the more luxurious accommodations available, including well-known hospitality brands? They come there for wildlife and love to stay close to nature, with an owner who can help them experience what they have come for.

Rajesh Shaw, Sundarbans

The same applies for another resort in the Sundarbans – though Rajesh Shaw, who runs the Eco Village, hates the 'resort' tag for what he has created. Rajesh, who went to the Sundarban mangrove forests as a tourist eight years ago, loved the place so much that he went back again and again – with his sister, other family members and friends. One day, he met an Englishman who advised him to make this his full-time job. He did, and set up Backpackers. Rajesh's love for the place – and its people – is obvious in everything he has done. In 2010, he bought a fishing trawler, and spent ₹6 lakh and five months to transform it into the cruise boat *Elmar* (Spanish for 'the deep', or the sea). The next year, he added another boat, *Para Siempre* ('forever' in Spanish). Rajesh and his nephew Mowgli began by putting up their guests on the boats – which has sleeping accommodation for 15 people - and in a village resort.

Then they bought a two-acre plot on the remote Satjelia island, where they built the Eco Village. Today, it has 14 thatched cottages, which can house 45 visitors. Rajesh met the villagers of the nearby Pakhiralay (Bengali for 'home of the birds') and earned their trust. He gave them various jobs like building the huts and the furniture, housekeeping and cooking the food – so the menu is always a tasty, spicy combination of local dishes. The kitchen is open for the guests to see their meal being cooked by the local women. "We had no designer or contractor, the villagers did everything," he explains.

"And it's all eco-friendly, using only local materials." Except, of course, for the bathroom fittings, the mattresses, bedsheets and blankets, and the mosquito nets. Backpackers also tries to buy most of its vegetables and fish from the local farmers and fishermen, and engages local folk artistes to present their art to guests. The island does not have electricity, so the Eco Village uses kerosene lanterns. The package that tourdesunderbans.com offers includes a jungle cruise by boat, besides road transfer from the company's office in Kolkata to the boat pier at Godkhali and back, the river crossing in either of the boats, stay, and food – morning tea, breakfast, lunch and dinner – both vegetarian and non-veg. Everything Rajesh earns is put back to build the place. "We just try to share the things that we did on our first trip and people like it," the site says. "Most of those activities are not conventional, like taking a dip in the village pond on a hot summer afternoon, or showing up uninvited at a local marriage on some remote island, or going to see a cock fight with the natives, or sitting around an oil lamp in a small hut on a cold winter night sipping the local rice liquor, listening to the experiences of the local honey collectors being attacked by tigers…"

Backpackers, which has been ranked third of 28 activities in Kolkata in international tourist portal TripAdvisor's Popularity Index, won a Certificate of Excellence in 2012 for its Tour de Sundarban day tours.

In your business check your context. If you are a student wanting to be an entrepreneur, check what you really love to do. What is the service you can provide which can have willing takers? A service which is currently not being serviced adequately, where the challenge is so acute that they are willing to pay more than what your costs are.

Make a list of such services required.

Checklist for you: List what you enjoy

See whether you can provide a service. Check who else is providing the service. What else can you enhance if a service already exists?

Can you join hands with the guy? Maybe pick up an equity stake? See what you will enjoy doing for the rest of your life. Money will follow in ways beyond your wildest imagination!

Interview: Harshvardhan Neotia, Chairman, Ambuja Neotia Group, Kolkata

Why did you move away from your family business of cement manufacture?

I entered the family business in 1984-85 when Ambuja Cements Ltd, which my father and uncle had set up, was being liquidated. I was overwhelmed with the scale of the operation, and wanted to do something smaller. Completely by chance, I got an opportunity to build a 20-apartment building of 20,000 square feet, on a plot of land that belonged to a family friend who was leaving Calcutta and moving to Bombay. My father and uncle were busy with the cement plant, so I didn't bother them asking for their advice. Also, it was a very small project – and besides, the family didn't have the knowledge to get into construction. Managerially, it was a completely new kettle of fish!

But you didn't have the domain knowledge, either.

No. I had got the ammonia-printed blueprints, in which I couldn't understand a thing! I found it a very humbling experience – completely illiterate workers can happily read drawings and work with them while, I, a B.Com. graduate, couldn't. The good thing was that I realized that I too could learn. I had Chakravarty babu, a diploma engineer, whom my architect recommended as the site supervisor. He was about 40 years old, I was around 25. He became my first tutor and explained everything to me. The project came out okay, and we even made more money than we had planned. We sold it to a Sindhi gentleman, who always wore a white safari suit, white shoes and glasses with a white-rimmed frame, and had a white pen in his pocket. But he would have only black coffee, black tea or a cola. "I wear only white, I drink only black!" he would say.

What other problems did you face in the beginning?

I had hired a car garage, which we converted into an air-conditioned office where I sat with two colleagues. But my white-suited buyer would not give me the cheque – he wanted to meet my father first. I had to take a firm stand and tell him that my father was not involved in my business.

What else did you do that was different?

My family has always been very involved in the fine arts, and I tried to bring aesthetics into my business. When I visited a mine, the manager was explaining how things work. But I imagined it filled with aqua-blue water, and was thinking what a beautiful site it would make for a hotel.

What learnings have you got from the business?

First, there is no definition of success. I have defined it for myself as the ability to get joy out of your work, make the world even one-millionth of a percent better. Second, I have learnt to make investments with passion, but detached enough to bring excellence. My philosophy has been, and is: "If it doesn't happen, it doesn't happen." Otherwise, I find, one can get no mental peace. Third, anxiety reduces the ability to do. A loss will only bother, not shatter, you. So I focus on what to do, not what to expect: as the verse from the Bhagawad Gita goes, "Karmanye vadhikaraste, Ma phaleshou kada chana" through which Krishna explains to Arjuna, who was not willing to fight the epic war of Mahabharata: "You have the right to perform your actions, but you are not entitled to the fruits of the actions."

This is not a Utopian concept – I have achieved it a bit. I believe in "enlightened self-interest': I do what I do because I am happy to do it, not for you or anyone else.

Case Study: Heady with Wine

Uma Chigurupati & C. Krishna Prasad, KRSMA Wines

When Uma Chigurupati got married and moved into her husband's home, she was shocked by the state of the spare bedroom: her new husband had turned it into a full-fledged winery. C. Krishna Prasad, now chairman and managing director of the ₹ 1,200-crore Granules India Ltd in Hyderabad, discovered wine when he was a student in Guntur, Andhra Pradesh. His father, a doctor, wanted him to follow in his footsteps – but Krishna had always had a fascination for 'doing something different' right from his childhood. So after meekly going through his B.Sc., he revolted and moved to Madras. After a number of good and failed businesses over the next eight years, he then asked himself, "Why don't I make wine?"

Growing up in the tobacco plantations of Guntur, Krishna had been exposed to a western environment, where 'scotch flowed' thanks to the large numbers of Britishers who lived there. He tasted his first wine at the local Bishop's home – and found it fascinating. So he got yeast from abroad, and began fermenting grapes in acid bottles. His first batch came out well, and he moved on to sparkling wine. He went to a five-star hotel, ordered champagne and brought the bottle back. He bought a cork sealer on a trip to the UK, and started in right earnest in 1981.

Uma, after her initial shock, started helping. But wine was still a hobby, not a bread-earning business. So Krishna got into pharmaceuticals and set up a company in which, too, he began doing something different: he pioneered the manufacture of pharmaceutical formulation intermediates (PFIs), when most Indian companies were making bulk drugs. Uma was a great help in this, too. "If I take up anything, I give it 100 percent," she says.

Pharma prospered, and the young couple had more time to indulge in another newly-discovered passion — for running. In 2003, they ran their first 10-km race to inspire people in their company, Granules India to live a healthy lifestyle. The experience was exhilarating. They started running half marathons, then full marathons. Krishna and Uma began running in some of the toughest marathons on the planet, and got into the Guinness Book of World Records in 2010 when they ran marathons across all seven continents – including Antarctica, through freezing winds, and in the North Pole at minus 34 degrees C. One stands out in their memories: the Medoc Marathon, which passes over scenic vineyards of Bordeaux and through fabled chateaux that produce some of the best wine in the world.

Every place the Chigurupatis travelled to, they savoured the wine. They also began visiting wineries, where they met leading oenologists and viticulturists, and amassed an amazing collection of wines. Now, the desire to make world-class wine grew stronger. They began considering — should they retire to the South of France and buy a vineyard there? A pharma customer in Italy had set up a small vineyard, and Krishna offered to take 5 per cent of it 'at any cost'. "But he said he couldn't sell, because he was planning to retire and go into wine!" They also visited Nashik in Maharashtra, famed as the wine capital of India – but didn't feel that it was the right place. Nothing clicked in other parts of country, including Himachal Pradesh, either.

And then Krishna heard of a farmer in Hampi, Karnataka, who was trying to grow wine grapes. "I went and met him, and liked the soil," he says. So did Uma, who is a qualified soil microbiologist and plant pathologist. The farmer was in financial difficulties, with his bank foreclosing on his loans – he was actually ripping up his vines. Krishna made him an offer then and there, took over the farm and replanted four hectares of the 12-hectare property in 2007.

"I'm not doing this for the money, that will always come," he explains. "I love good wine!" So does Uma, who has developed an interest in viticulture and then tasting. Over the years, she too has developed a discerning palate to differentiate good wines. There is a market for these in India, Krishna says: "It's my personal conviction, without reservation, that there is a need for premium wines here. People are now understanding the difference."

The passion has them both in its grip. While Krishna is at the farm as often as he can, it's Uma who makes it a point to drive six hours every weekend and goes around tasting grapes from every row of vines to make sure they taste just right. "I spend 15 days in Hampi every season, she's there for 45 days," he says.

The couple has spared no effort: they used regulated deficit irrigation to make up for the lack of rainfall and an organic-specific fertigation regime. Every step has their personal touch, from deciding the time of pruning the vines to harvesting the grapes – on 1 January every year, finishing by 9-o'clock in the morning so that the temperature is just right — then selecting the fine-grain French oak barrels, in which the wine is aged and putting it into bottles imported from France with labels from Australia, capsules from

Spain and natural cork from the US. They truly believe that 'the best fertiliser for the vineyard is the owners' footsteps'.

At KRSMA – the brand, which is a blend of their first names — there are no recipes. Each vintage is different from the next, because it's the grapes that make the difference to the wine. No wonder, then, that the four varietals they stick to have won so many awards: the Chardonnay of 2013, Cabernet Sauvignon of 2012 and Sauvignon Blanc of 2013 have won the double gold, gold and silver medals respectively, at the China Wine and Spirit Awards 2013; the Sauvignon Blanc of 2012 the bronze medal at the New Zealand International Wine Show 2012; and the Chardonnay was commended at the recently held International Wine Challenge 2014. Krishna and Uma truly love not only wine, but what they are doing.

An organization is the reflection of the promoter's energy

You can recreate everything you have lost.

All you need is enthusiasm says Sanjay Thakker — the creator of corporate SSY (Siddha Samadhi Yoga) which teaches people at workplaces to live joyously and contribute meaningfully. He holds several workshops on leadership and is a life coach.

At every stage of the business an entrepreneur's energy will be different. He begins mostly on nothing. Even if he is from a moneyed background he has nothing much to lose as others' expectations would be in line with his relative lack of experience. So he is standing on nothing. In a rags-to-riches story, too, he has nothing to lose – but everything to gain. This is also the time when there is a lot of enthusiasm. There is no history of success. There is only one thing to do: learn as much as you can, as fast as you can. You are hungry for everything. New clients, experiences, new team members, setting up an office. In other words, your ego has not yet developed to the point where you think you know everything. When you have already reached the "already always listening" mode — a Leadership Training Programme by Werner Erhard — where he talks about 'Already Always Listening'. This is when you are working from past experience and not paying attention.

When does an organization thrive? When its promoter's energy is at its most enthusiastic. When everybody in the organization is bubbling with energy. When the team is enthused. Nothing is impossible. It is fun. Every day there are new learnings. How does all this become possible? The entrepreneur's vision, the energy he brings to every relationship, every transaction plays a large part. The business is thriving when the entrepreneur is focused and enthusiastic about it. "How can I do it?" is the question he is asking rather than "why me?" He is a leader in the truest sense where every day is new and brimming with possibilities.

How can I improve this business? Why should a customer buy from me? How can I shorten the 'to market' time? What is the learning from the last failure? These are the mental conversations he is having with himself.

However, there does come a time in an entrepreneur's life when his or her enthusiasm starts waning. This happens normally when you are not learning and you want to bask in security or in your past glory rather than going back to basics or going after new adventures. Remember, a business is like riding a cycle. N.R. Narayanamurthy, founder of Infosys, has said something very interesting: "At every stage of Infosys I changed first..."

What is the meaning of this? As your organization moves into the next level you should move ahead first. The organization follows. You have created the next level. It doesn't exist if you are not yourself ready to go there first. This needs mental preparation where you have to take bigger risks, go that extra mile, travel to distant shores. At this juncture what is important is: how is the owner of the business feeling about his enterprise? How is he treating it? Is he providing care, nourishment, attention to it? How would you take care of a child? How would you take care of a plant?

This is all exchange of energy. We need to energize our relationships every day. Let's look at marriage or a parent-child relationship. It needs to be nurtured every day. You need to add value to it if you want the relationship to thrive and grow, much like a plant. But most of us are guilty of not 'giving it enough juice'.

A business is the same. Once we decide to provide the x service to y customers, we have to continuously see how we can enhance the experience. But sadly, we get dejected at the first sign of so-called rejection.

Rejection of creatives in an ad agency is the cause for the greatest grief. Why? Because art guys identify themselves as Art guys whose creativity is beyond question. If they changed the context, and began seeing themselves instead as solution providers through art would they feel rejected? 'My design' would be replaced by 'design solutions' — and they would keep designing the solution till it is accepted by both parties. But the minute we face rejection, what is it that is likely to be going through our minds?

Why am I in this business?

I slog day in and day out and what do I get?

If my client knows everything why doesn't he do it himself?

This is it, I throw in the towel!

Oh, why me?

Is it my bad luck?

All these thoughts clutter our mind and drag our energy and enthusiasm to rock bottom. If this happens all the time, we are no longer focusing on the business. We are not focusing on our customers and how we can serve them best. All we are then focused on is 'poor me' (the 'poor me' syndrome or the victim mentality).

If this happens continuously we are going to hit rock-bottom pretty quickly.

Let's look at the way you started your business. You were bursting with enthusiasm, energy, excitement. Everything was possible. The only No in your vocabulary translated into 'Nothing is impossible'. But human nature is such that sometimes we do get tired, satisfied or pretty full up with what we have achieved. There may be a reluctance to learn something new. This is also the time you may notice that things are slowly spiralling downward. Unfortunately, many times, such downward trends are so small in the beginning that we do not even notice them. If left unattended it will be a slow dance to death.

Interestingly, you will notice the downward spiral only if you are alert and aware. If you are too busy drowning your own sorrows — literally and figuratively — you may not even notice that nobody is growing in the organization. You will notice that somebody is lagging behind only if you are ahead of the curve. Ironic, isn't it?

Check how the accounts department becomes slow and lethargic in making bills, in collection. Check for falling customer service standards. Check for shoddy jobs delivered to customers; poor response time. All this is a reflection of your own energy. You can conduct this experiment with yourself. The day you are full of beans everything will go very well. Customers are happy; the team seems to be charged up. But the day you are disgruntled, things don't go your way at all.

The enthusiasm, ability to learn, and forward thinking you bring to the table will rub off on your team as well. This is true for any manager who has to manage a bunch of people, or even at home with your family. The entrepreneur's energy has to be high at all times. Challenges and a mountain of tasks should excite him. Multi-tasking should make him giddy with exhilaration. Again, this book is meant for people who need to manage at least 100 people. Smaller mom-

and-pop stores can definitely be run in a much less demanding fashion. But still some of these rules will apply there too — maybe in a miniature version.

Harish Bijoor, CEO,
Harish Bijoor Consults Inc, Bangalore

Let's read some experiences which connect to both, Principles 1 and 2, about how some great start-ups slowed down, then interestingly picked themselves up, soon enough.

Entrepreneurship sure is a bug, says Harish Bijoor, brand-strategy specialist and CEO of the eponymous Harish Bijoor Consults Inc. brand consultancy in Bangalore who, in an earlier avatar, created 'Tata Kapi'. "Entrepreneurship happened accidentally to me," says Harish, who started his career at Hindustan Lever and then moved on to work with the Tatas. "I was just about to take up a big assignment as President, Marketing in India's biggest telecom entity, and making a quick trip to the US before putting in my papers for the job I was in. On the second leg of the flight, from London to New York, I found myself sitting next to the Senior Director of a Washington DC-based venture capitalist on the prowl. This was First Class, and the Dom Perignon was flowing in-flight. Two glasses later we got talking. To end a long story, by the time the flight landed in New York, Tim had convinced me to visit their offices in Manhattan and give the job a shot. The offer was a simple one: float a private-label consulting business in India, get funded by the VC firm he represented, look after its existing businesses in Hong Kong, and people this whole operation with branding and marketing oriented minds. India was to be my own territoryand all of SE Asia, the UK, and the Middle East was to be theirs, managed by me."

Having got over his fear of "no more monthly salary cheques if I bit into this", Harish did indeed, bite. Eleven years later, heading a team of 91 people, Harish says he had 'lots of downs' in business. "When I started, I had all of two people to supervise – down from the 2200 people I was looking after in my previous organization, one which employed 22,000 people," he says. "All of a sudden I was everything. I had nobody to delegate anything to. I had to control cash flows carefully. If I didn't do that piece of work right, my people's next month's remuneration was in question. For two years we managed just three clients. What a far cry from the 141 we manage today! Life certainly was tough. I had my doubts many a time whether I had done right in quitting the possibility of a cushy big — name corporate job. Today, of course, I don't regret that."

Y. Rajeev Reddy, founder chairman and managing director, Country Club India Ltd, says "I'm not a high-profile guy - I prefer a Nano, not a BMW or Mercedes-Benz!" He had to overcome many challenges in the initial stages of setting up what has now become India's biggest chain of family clubs, where its members occupied 80,000 room nights in 2012 alone.

That was the year in which Country Club spread its wings to Bangalore. "I could have just stayed in Hyderabad and been happy like many others who started businesses there around that time, but I wanted to take my company pan-India – and global," Rajeev says. So he made a presentation to J.H. Patel, then the Chief Minister of Karnataka. "But I didn't ask for any Government favours!" he clarifies. Today, he has 11 clubs in the state, seven of which are in Bangalore.

Another major problem was in Bombay (now Mumbai), where it was difficult to get property even then. "Putting your stamp there is not easy, it's a very tough market," Rajeev says. Chance put him next to movie superstar Rajesh Khanna on a flight, who advised him: "Bombay will give you only one chance – so think big." He followed the tip in some detail - "I booked the entire Renaissance hotel and gave away champagne and room nights," he recalls. It worked, and he signed on many new members – and 'put his stamp' on the city. "So many people have disappeared from business," he says. "Only one in 10 survives."

Achal Bakeri, CMD of Ahmedabad-based air coolers giant Symphony Ltd, is one of the survivors. Achal had moved out of his father's business of real estate development and into his uncle's textile unit because he "no longer wanted to be a cog in the wheel", and set up his own unit. Why did he decide to make air coolers? "I shifted, and had to install these in some parts of my new house that weren't suitable for air-conditioning," he explains. "The quality of the equipment available on the market – the so-called 'desert coolers', with the khus sheets and a huge noisy fan – was bad. I decided to create an air cooler that looked sleek like an air-conditioner, but cost only a fraction of an AC. It was a truly aspirational product."

He started developing a product around Deepavali in 1987, and launched it in March 1988. He showed it to his family and friends, who liked it and encouraged him. The entire production of the newly — incorporated Symphony Pvt. Ltd was sold in the first summer, bringing Achal a revenue of ₹ 25-30 lakh. He went from success to success, appointed dealers and advertised on national television in 1990. "My advertising budget was more than the turnover of the previous year!" he says. The company built its own factory in 1991 and went public in 1994.

Achal's ambition, and a well-wisher's advice, led him to get into a whole range of other products – "Why restrict myself to one season, summer?" he argued. So Symphony started manufacturing converters, hot-water geysers, water purifiers and washing machines. Not even one of them succeeded in the marketplace, and the company's entire net worth was eroded by 2001, when it became a BIFR (Bureau of Industrial and Financial Restructuring) case with what he calls "a mountain of debt". His world had crashed. He remembers those days with a shudder: "I went through hell. I can't describe it in words!"

But refusing to say die, Achal reworked his business strategy and exited all the other products to re-focus on his cash cow. From 2002 on, Symphony became a single-product company again, and clawed back to solvency. "I began repaying the financial institutions, and finished by 2007. In fact, I paid the last instalment three months before the date I had committed," he says. By June 2008, the company was back in the black and out of BIFR's purview. Today it is the largest manufacturer of air coolers in the world, making more than half a million units – from small portable machines to huge industrial ones — every year. It has an annual turnover of ₹1100 crore; its market capitalization, which had dipped to a penny-stock level, has zoomed to ₹1700 crore. "I want to sell a million units, in many more countries," he adds.

What kept Achal going? "Pride in myself!" he says. "I didn't go to my family for a bailout. My two daughters were in school, but I tried not to let my problems touch them though I downgraded my own lifestyle. I sold my Standard Motors' Rover Montego and began using a hand-me-down car which I had bought for an executive, and stopped flying Business Class." Since then, the upward curve has continued. In 2008 itself, Symphony acquired a 70-year-old air-cooler manufacturer in the US. "Opportunity knocked, so I struck and took the plunge!" he grins. "The experience of our Indian restructuring came in handy there, though their high-capex business model was different from ours. But we turned it around after a lot of financial engineering and cost reduction, and made it reasonably profitable."

Is there a way to bring back enthusiasm in your life? What could be business rejuvenation for an entrepreneur?

Bring back that excitement with which you started. Start afresh as if it is the first day of your business.

Go and listen to some great thinkers and speakers. Do a couple of short management programmes. Identify your weak areas. If it is strategic thinking, read up W. Chan Kim and Renée Mauborgne's book *Blue Ocean Strategy*. If it is operations, attend a Verne Harnish session — Strategy & Execution.

If it is some motivation you require, attend *Chicken Soup for the Soul* co-author Jack Canfield's session on Success Principles.

If it is lateral thinking which you are in need of, Edward de Bono is whom I would strongly recommend.

You have to invest in improving yourself. Most of these programmes cost ₹ 25,000 or so. But they are well worth it. You will always pick up a couple of things which will help you move to the next level.

But learning also needs enthusiasm. Conversely, once you start learning something new some dormant parts of your brain get activated — which helps you see things in a new perspective. This in turn helps you to realign yourself to your goals. Your enthusiasm comes back. You start in the morning with renewed energy and focus.

Alternatively, take up something new like painting, long-distance running, music, or singing lessons. Do something you have never done before. Travel. The greatest remedy to bring back your enthusiasm is to get out of your comfort zone and experience different things, eat different food. Travel in public transport in a foreign country where you don't know the language. Go to a bar and have a drink with the locals. You will start experiencing life from a different perspective.

Exercise

Gauge your energy level: how do you feel on Monday?

What is your enthusiasm level? How do you feel when you have to meet a new client? When you have to meet dealers/distributors. Investors. Bankers. This fires fresh neurons in the brain – which aids new ways of thinking.

How do you feel when you are making the projections for the quarter or year?

Tip: Apart from spending quiet time, go for a walk in a beautiful garden. The walking activates the *chakras* in the feet. It rejuvenates you. A fresh mind can always think of more ideas.

Interview: Chandra Mohan, Padmashri, Founder Chairman, Punjab Tractors Ltd (PTL), and Author, *Making Entrepreneurs: Lessons from a Lifetime*

What was the main factor that drove you to face any number of skeptics and build India's first indigenous tractor?

I was young. I had a good, enthusiastic team with me. All around us were those who were saying we couldn't do it. They told me I was crazy! *"Banega nahi! Agar banega bhi, to chalega nahi!"* they said. We proved them all wrong. I believe firmly that there is a significant difference between entrepreneurship and small business: it lies in innovation and high risk-taking ability, which together lead to far larger and faster wealth creation. And I have proved it with PTL and the 100% Indian Swaraj brand of tractor that my team and I designed and built from scratch in a national lab 47 years ago, then mass-produced and marketed against the best of CKD-based global brand names. And risk is at its highest when you are launching a drastic innovation in product or production technology in an intensely competitive field, like we did.

So you define an entrepreneur as someone who has necessarily to take risks?

I believe that an entrepreneur is someone who perceives the opportunity to use his knowledge to innovate, create and build something new of recognized value. But risk is inevitable in this, so it is natural to try and create entrepreneurs when their ability to take it is at its highest, and their innovative minds are full of energy and ripe for a career on their own. That moment is straight after graduation in professional courses – so the risk period would get drastically reduced if the major preparatory work for setting up the enterprise is completed before graduation. This in turn boils down to selecting potential entrepreneurs soon after students opt for professional streams of their choice. Grooming them and planning for establishment of enterprises should proceed in step with the remaining years of their professional education.

How would you look back at your career as an entrepreneur?

I'm still an entrepreneur. At the age of 80 plus, I can proudly say that I have been one for the last 49 years of my professional innings of 58 years. My focus has always been on technology and innovation. I filed a patent in photovoltaics in 2008.

Have you always done things which other people describe as 'crazy'?

I decided to quit the Indian Railways after 12 years to join CMERI, a CSIR Lab in Durgapur. Many people felt that was a crazy move. Then, I got involved in the R&D for a tractor tailored specifically for the use — and abuse — of Indian farmers and the rough-and-tough agricultural conditions in India.

Why was that so strange, wanting to make an indigenous product?

Remember this was in the mid-60s. It was total heresy! Even when you look for engineering products today in 2013, imported know-how dominates the mindset of Indian entrepreneurs. No wonder, our Swaraj was rejected at the highest levels of the land in favour of Czech technology, even after five years of systematic slog during which three prototypes were cleared after 1500 hours of field tests and mandatory testing by the Government of India's own Tractor Testing Station in Madhya Pradesh.

So how did your project get off the ground in the face of such opposition?

We got a white knight in shining armour. Tejendra Khanna, then the young MD of Punjab State Industrial Development Corporation (PSIDC), decided to license the know-how. He even invited me and my core five-man team to help PSIDC set up the project. PTL was duly incorporated on 28 May, 1970. As a professionally managed company, it has been on the Stock Market since Day 1.

We rolled out the Swaraj within the promised budget and time frame, then expanded capacity, launched new products and entered allied lines like LCVs, forklifts and seating systems, and adopted Total Quality Management as a business strategy. The company became debt-free in 1991, and subsequent growth was all financed internally. The pace of expansion and modernization was stepped up and capacity was raised to 60,000 including a new green-field facility. We were also the largest exporter till 1997. Sales crossed the 50,000 mark in 1998 and revenues touched ₹ 900 crore. The journey had begun in 1972 with a total equity of only ₹ 1.1 crore.

Revenues of the Swaraj Group of companies (flagship PTL and its subsidiaries Swaraj Mazda, Swaraj Engines and Swaraj Automotives) totalled ₹ 1500 crore in 1998. All the companies were on the dividend list. The Group had 4000 direct employees and had created 16,000 indirect jobs in ancillaries. And it is still the largest employer in the State of Punjab, though the ownership structure has changed.

After those great achievements, why did you decide to quit PTL?

I was 65 years old in December 1997. It was then that I called it a day with PTL and the Swaraj Group. It had been a long journey - beginning with framing the specifications of Swaraj in 1965 and covering every variety of enterprise — big and small; manufacturing, service and non-profit; and both successes and failures. Of course there have been failures on the way — but they have not deterred me from sculpting new dreams. Innovation is seemingly an organic component of my blood-stream.

What is your book about?

Making Entrepreneurs... is a critical self-analysis in search of a process for identifying potential entrepreneurs out of students pursuing higher professional education and then grooming them for setting up their projects along with their professional courses... and mentoring them all the way through till they are ready to commence implementation as they graduate. Yes, there are definite attractions in a safe job with a guaranteed monthly salary. But I have been searching for a solution to this — that led me to look into my own journey as a pioneering technology-led professional entrepreneur.

Case Study: Booked!

T.N. Shanbhag, Strand

T. Narayan Shanbhag, who started Mumbai's iconic Strand Book Stall in November 1948 and ran it till he died in 2009 at the age of 85, was the personification of the principle this chapter enunciates. Here is an extract from a biography written in 2003.

Bookselling for him was never limited to 'trading' but "has been a pursuit of sharing the great human experiences either in Arts or Sciences that are stored in book form." He is the first bookseller felicitated with the Padmashree. But more important for him is the long list of his patrons beginning with Pandit Nehru and the three generations of book lovers whose visit to Fort in south Mumbai is not complete without a peep into his shop.

If Shanbhag's life-story is incredible, replete with frequent brushes with celebrities from across the world, the origin of the bookshop has had a no less dramatic genesis. As a college student, he had gone to Strand Cinema to watch a classic movie, 'Cheaper by the Dozen.' During the interval, an empty corner in the cinema theatre seized his attention and it struck him as the right place to open a small book kiosk. He neither had any knowledge of the bookselling trade or the margins involved – nor did he have the capital to launch his venture. He had a meagre ₹ 450 saved up from his scholarships which he had won solely on his outstanding academic performance.

With his resolve to open a bookshop, he straightaway boarded a BEST bus, reached Tardeo and called on 'Strand' owner Keki Modi, who owned 55 other cinemas in the country, with his outlandish proposal. The business giant was highly amused with the young man's enthusiasm though he was initially sceptical as Shanbhag had no experience of the trade. Finally, the young man's earnestness won him over and Modi granted him the space. Shanbhag's fortune had started smiling. Sensing his lack of finances, Modi got a kiosk built to Shanbhag's specifications in that corner. This kiosk, which had such a modest beginning, has now metamorphosed into one of the most reputed bookshops of India, with an equally flourishing branch at Bangalore, looked after by his daughter Vidya Virkar.

When a reader becomes a seller, the activity transcends into a spiritual experience which has no boundaries. Shanbhag epitomizes this transformation. No wonder, the selection for the maiden display of books within the confines of the kiosk was exceptional. His first adventure was to buy 500 copies of the first volume of Winston Churchill's *War Memoirs*. Shanbhag's first customer at the Strand was an American. He still remembers the day vividly. It was 20th November 1948 and the visitor was Richard Burton, chairman of Standard Vacuum Oil Company, one of the eight greatest MNCs in the world then. Burton was pleasantly surprised when he was offered a 20-per-cent discount on the *Memoirs*, published only a few weeks earlier. He was surprised because this was the first time when any bookseller offered such a hefty discount. Equally impressive was Shanbhag's sales pitch. Gradually, the word-of-mouth publicity did the trick and people started taking notice of the kiosk.

As sales boomed, Shabhag was able to buy more good books in large quantities and every time he got better discounts from publishers, he gave away the extra discounts to the reader by keeping about 10 per cent, to cover the overheads. This was a self-imposed discipline. To give an example, the latest book of Stephen Hawking's, *The Universe in a Nutshell* is being sold at ₹625 against the printed price of ₹2460, received from the USA by air freight.

Shri Yashwantrao Chavan became one of his earliest customers and also a great well-wisher, practically within a few weeks of opening the shop. He was a voracious reader of outstanding books. The second early leader who became a great well-wisher was Union finance minister and Nehru's right-hand man, T.T. Krishnamachari.

Born in a lower-middle-class family in Mangalore district on 26th August 1925, Shanbhag bought the *Complete Works of Swami Vivekananda* from Advaita Ashram, Calcutta, for ₹27. This was his first acquisition. Swamiji, perhaps the greatest humanist produced in the last several centuries, continues to inspire him greatly.

Shanbhag became a passionate reader at an early age and by the time he was 13, he had read most of the classics from the high school library. As he joined St. Xavier's College in Bombay for his BA, he read Plato, Aristotle and other great works. He had to work part-time to support his studies but persevered through grit and determination. From his hard-earned savings, he began buying Penguins and Pelicans which were an "English Library" containing 20,000 titles including famous fiction as well as great books by philosophers, astronomers, historians, economists and thinkers. He was fond of browsing before buying books. Once, he was rudely treated by a salesman for browsing through the latest lot of Penguins and Pelicans in one of the largest bookshops in Bombay at the time. Shanbhag felt that the bookshop was going against the spirit of Saraswati, the Goddess of knowledge. He also believed that knowledge is neither to be sold nor bought as Gurudev Tagore wrote in his Geetanjali. – "Where knowledge is free". In other words, it is to be shared. Giving discounts was an experience in sharing. Shanbhag walked to the nearby Prince of Wales Museum. He sat under a shady tree to find a way to give expression to these ideals. Finally, he decided that he himself would become a bookseller where any reader should not only be free to browse but get a book of his choice at the best possible low price.

Shanbhag told veteran journalist Dom Moraes in an interview, "I am wedded to the printed word. Nothing else is sacred to me. I have my own perceptions of what is fundamental. The purpose of a book shop is to allow free access to all those who are interested in the printed word. The bookseller's business is to choose what he considers to be the best books and make them available." He told him that a great bookseller and a publisher came from the same class of people who society respected greatly. They vibed in a similar way and he felt that it was his privilege to belong to that profession.

Shanbhag introduced to India many outstanding authors from different countries. He was the first bookseller to secure 1,000 copies of Andre Malraux's *Voices of Silence* as well as Robert Musil's *Man Without Qualities*. Authors like Franz Kafka, Karel Kapek became known mostly because of him. Manya Harari told him on a visit to Bombay while having dinner with him that she had just translated a smuggled manuscript from the USSR, called *Dr Zhivago*, by Boris Pasternak. If ever there was a masterpiece, this was one of them, she said. Shanbhag was the only bookseller to order 1,000 copies while almost all other booksellers in India thought it was the life of a doctor and did not bother to order. The availability of *Dr Zhivago* attracted the attention of Who's Who in India and brought many intellectuals to Strand Book Stall.

Material success was bound to follow. Of course, Shanbhag established not only financial stability for the business but achieved his ambition of building up of a tremendous reputation. He and his staff have ensured that nothing happens that can affect this trust. Shanbhag believes that to be an 'archetypal' bookseller, he should meet great authors who are the fountainhead of creativity as well as great publishers who would not only enlighten him on the technology and the economics of publishing but throw light on several related subjects like ideology and subject category. In this pursuit, he met Sir Allen Lane, the founder of Penguins and Pelicans, who had started his venture in similar circumstances as Shanbhag. Lane's initial was a meagre 100 sterling pounds. He started with an ideology like replacing hardbacks and making books cheaper.

One day, Nani Palkhivala unexpectedly breezed into his bookshop and put into his hands a manuscript called *We, the People*. When he pointed out that he was a bookseller and not a publisher, Palkhivala countered by saying, "Wherever I go, I hear such wonderful comments about you, including from the Chief Justice of the Supreme Court." The book was eventually published by Shanbhag and it sold over 50,000 copies. Another occasion was the visit of great architect and theoretician, Charles Correa, who came and did the same. The book was called *The New Landscape* (for the 21st *century*). Not only did the book sell well but he received an equivalent of the Nobel Prize from the Emperor of Japan. Both these great souls were

Shanbhag's customers first, friends next and of course, well-wishers. He got the books sold internationally. He argues that no two books are the same commodity and each one appeals to only a certain reader. Therefore, anyone who accepts a book should know how to handle it.

"His personality and idealism have left a unique imprint on the book trade, both in India and abroad," feels his daughter Vidya Virkar, partner of Strand Book Stall, Bangalore. About her father, she says, "I feel truly blessed to have a dad like him. There is an adage which says your children are not your belongings. Enjoy them, for they have been gifted to you but for a little while. As Shanbhag's daughter, I would turn this adage to fit my father!"

[Taken with permission from *SHAN of Book Selling* by Dilip Chaware. Published by Vishwa Samvad Kendra 2003]

———⁂———

Focus, focus, focus

Keep an eye on the business at all times. On customer satisfaction, innovations, profitability, value, top line, bottom line, clients, vendors...

..Add value to your business every day.

Let me narrate an incident which will resonate in every business owner's heart.

I was returning from a meeting when I stopped at one of the coffee bars which dot the freeway between Mumbai and Pune for a cuppa... I ordered a latte. For ₹ 72 including taxes. When I went to pick up my order I realized that for ₹ 70 I could have had a cheese toast along with a cappuccino. I asked the counter guy whether he could change the order. Of course he couldn't. This was completely understandable. My question however, was why he did not suggest this to me in the first place. As per the textbook and what is taught in school he was right. But from a business perspective it was a failed transaction from the customer satisfaction angle. Honestly, I was pretty annoyed.

Cut to another scenario in south Mumbai. We went to a very well-known and popular vegetarian restaurant where the toilets have televisions. Guess why? The restaurant is located near the famous Dalal Street. So plenty of traders may be coming in for lunch. I am sure the sets have been installed to add value, so customers can have a bite without missing any of the action of what is happening at the stock market even when they have to use the washroom. Amazing value! These are the small things which translate to adding value to your customers.

I have coined my own meaning for value. I would loosely define value as 'that which is not asked, not expected, not contracted but that which is delivered in any transaction thereby delighting the receiver'. Harking back to the coffee bar example — if the employee was pulled up he would not technically be in the wrong... He cannot be fired for that particular transaction but at the same time he need not be promoted. This is the difference when you add value.

In today's very competitive scenario where almost everything is commoditized, what can be the differentiators? Can delighting your customers in unexpected ways be the answer? After all this adds to the experience, doesn't it?

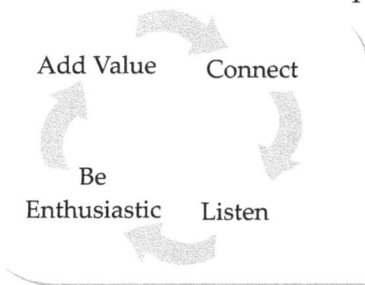

Add Value   Connect

Be
Enthusiastic   Listen

I now have a new rule which of course I am still mastering. When you go for a meeting think of only four things:

Simple! Of course, being well-versed with your presentation or whatever it is you are in the meeting for is a hygiene factor.

Let's elaborate a little more on each of them.

Focus on customer satisfaction = delivering value as defined

There are times when our team members wonder why they are not growing in their jobs despite following all the rules, and doing all the right things. My answer to this is simple. Add value. For doing the prescribed job all you will have is the job. For adding value the organization will certainly take you to the next level. If that organization does not recognize you somebody else surely will. For an employee or entrepreneur who adds value, the sky is the limit and no recession can really touch him or her. Sometimes in our line of business we get disgruntled because despite working like donkeys there is no appreciation from the client. My answer is again simple. For working sincerely we still have his business — but to delight him add value. Give him something which is not in the contract, which is unexpected, which he has not thought about.

Focus on Innovation

Again, this is a by-product of customer satisfaction. If you continue to do the same thing you will continue to get the same results.

The greatest innovations did not happen because people simply followed what was there. In a business continuous innovation is a must. Measuring those innovations is even better. Innovation is an oft-repeated word and I suspect most people cannot connect with it. I would put it very simply as follows, with a practical example.

Innovation in a business is doing the same thing in a different manner to produce different – and better – results. Let us take a household example. In every traditional south Indian home there was a grinding stone to make idli and dosa which were the staple items for breakfast. One smart manufacturer studied the women slogging every morning and came out with a grinder which took out the sweat (literally) and toil from the daily breakfast. Grinders were still cumbersome; so they innovated and came out with mixers.

But still the south Indian housewife was not ecstatic as the mixer had its limitations in grinding parboiled rice — a necessity for idli. So the manufacturer, not one to give up, came out with table-top grinders. Now there exists in the market a compact grinder which occupies almost the same space as a mixer / grinder. This is innovation. What does the table-top do? The same job — grinding. But how does it benefit the housewife or lady of the house?

- Cuts the time
- Reduces effort
- Saves space

The family can now enjoy a traditional breakfast more often.

The lady of the house is happy as she is taking care of her family's health, nutrition and taste while delivering a traditional breakfast in a modern convenient setting. Win-win, I would say.

Now let us examine our own businesses.

Focus on systems and processes.

We have many antiquated business practices which we all follow. They are no longer relevant — so why do we follow them? A yearly review of all systems and processes along with a review of teams, clients, targets, sales and revenue is a good idea.

A new revenue stream may emerge from this. More on this later as we have a whole section devoted to it.

Where can we do simple innovation in our own businesses?

Can we be more innovative in payment collection? Start billing the customer as soon as the job is done instead of after 15 days. Different industries follow different methodologies. So please check what is relevant for you.

In manpower management there are different formations:

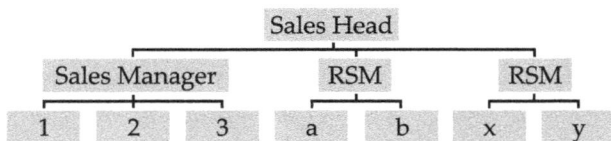

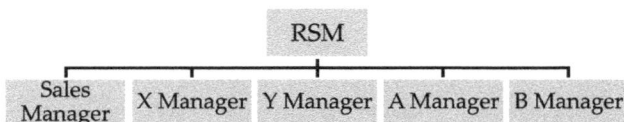

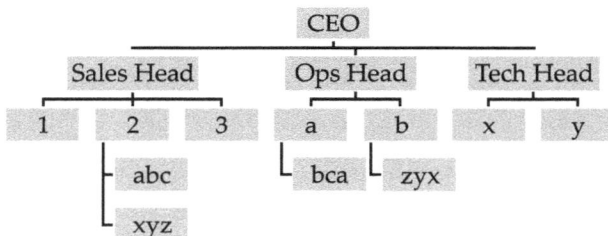

```
                        Sales Head
        ┌────────────────────┼────────────────┐
   Sales Manager            RSM              RSM
   ┌─────┼─────┐         ┌────┴────┐      ┌────┴────┐
   1     2     3         a         b      x         y
```

```
                        RSM
      ┌──────────┬──────────┬──────────┬──────────┐
   Sales      X Manager   Y Manager  A Manager  B Manager
   Manager
```

```
                        CEO
        ┌────────────────────┬────────────────┐
   Sales Head             Ops Head         Tech Head
   ┌─────┼─────┐         ┌────┴────┐      ┌────┴────┐
   1     2     3         a         b      x         y
       ├─ abc         └─ bca   └─ zyx
       └─ xyz
```

Different team formations

A two-man team, hierarchical structure, or one team member with 3 people. Single one-man shows.....depending on what the industry is, team formation can be different. We do not need to follow anybody's method. One of the biggest fallacies humans subscribe to is to do what others are doing and make it your rule. Have you ever questioned whether it is your rule? Is that rule or process still relevant? Why are you following it? How is it benefiting you or your company in any way?

Another area of innovation can be the product itself. Sony invented the Walkman and created a new product category. But unfortunately the iPod was created by Apple and not Sony. The rules of the game in business are being rewritten every day. The market leader of yesterday can be a complete laggard tomorrow. The Nokia handset business has got bought over by Microsoft. Even four years ago, could we ever have imagined this scenario? The sunrise industry of today can be and will be a mature business tomorrow. So in this very dynamic scenario how does an entrepreneur take care of his business? One of the answers is to innovate. I am beginning to think that what is required is a start-up culture in at least one division of the company which can keep innovating something new. Of course, the win is when an existing old-world department starts thinking in exciting new ways. Imagine how your company will be rejuvenated.

The need of the day is to also give a boost to companies which have been around for many years and are now floundering. This phenomenon happened in our own company. Five years ago we set up an incubation unit for digital marketing and advertising. As we all know the digital business is very RoI driven since everything is measurable. You know where the audience comes from, what his behaviour is, why he has clicked, on what content he clicked, whether he filled up your form or where he went without filling up your form. Our traditional advertising business, which was the parent company, started thinking, why don't we also start thinking in terms of measurability? Why not beef up our regular offering and make it more RoI (Return of Investment) driven for clients? This created a different result-oriented mindset in the company. These are early days yet. But still, a younger division with young people can sometimes breathe new life into an older set-up too. I always believe it is better to destroy and recreate ourselves before market forces compel us to do so.

Indian Map Service (IMS) in Jodhpur is yet to cross the digital divide, but it has been innovating over the past quarter century to provide what it perceives as a valuable service required by its target audience, mainly tourists. Dr R.P. Arya, who was chief cartographer at Tamilnadu Printers & Traders which subsequently became TTK

Dr R.P. Arya,
Indian Map Service (IMS), Jodhpur

Maps, and his son Anshuman are constantly expanding the range of their products. Today, with a range of world, national, state and city maps – with a variety of intra-city sectional maps thrown in – they have maps and guides that cater to corporate houses, hotels, tourism departments, travel agencies and the common traveller. IMS even offers customised, multi-lingual maps – for instance, it created one for Hindustan Petroleum to show the location of its LPG cooking gas dealers in various cities. "Thorough knowledge of the subject is a big advantage," says Dr Arya, who is the only professional geographer trained in cartography at Jodhpur University and learned how to make maps in the erstwhile pre-unification West Germany way back in 1966.

Devanshu & Rajesh Gandhi, MDs,
Vadilal Industries Ltd, Ahmedabad

In Ahmedabad, Rajesh Gandhi, MD of ice-cream manufacturer Vadilal Industries Ltd, joined his family business immediately after completing college, and has taken it from being a small shop his grandfather had opened in 1907 to becoming a national business with a turnover of over ₹ 1 crore. "It was a purely local brand when I joined," he says. "My brother Shailesh and I took it to the next level, to the outskirts of the city; then, in steps, all over Gujarat, to the neighbouring states, and now national. Everything had to be reinvented, there is no fixed formula." It took the Gandhi brothers three years of trial and error to build India's first refrigerated vehicle to carry their product, as the imported ones they could have bought otherwise involved big hassles for getting an import licence, then an import duty of 30 percent. Moving on beyond ice cream to other frozen foods, Vadilal diversified into processed foods in 1992, and now exports to 40 countries. What kept them going? "Risk-taking ability is very important," Rajesh says. "And support from the entrepreneur's family members."

Focus also on top line, bottom line and cash flow.

It is not enough to focus only on the top line and bottom line, we realized rather late in the day. What is most important is the free cash a company throws up every year. More importantly, where is the cash? Is it with the Income Tax department in terms of disputed refunds? Is it with your customers as debts or is it in any unproductive asset like a godown which is not being used?

With much pain we finally realized in our company that cash flow is what really matters at the end of the day. Warren Buffett has been preaching this for years.

There is a humorous saying which is very true and the sooner an entrepreneur learns it, the better off he is:

> Top line is vanity;
>
> Bottom line is sanity;
>
> Cash flow is reality.

For the first several years focusing on top line is good. It is classic business practice. Much like what the internet companies of the early 2000s did and what e-commerce companies of 2013-14 like Flipkart, etc are doing. You need to grow the company. But there comes a time when if you do not start focusing on the bottom line you will soon be history. There again comes a time when only bottom line is not relevant. It is good for your investors, bankers, for the market - but the reality is, have you collected all the money which is your bottom line, or is it in the market? Think about it — if you have been in business for 20 years there will come a time when you want to see where the cash is.

The last count I did, I could see where the cash for my company was. Most of it was with Income Tax as TDS; some was with Service Tax as we have to pay in advance and we need to collect from clients later; some more of course was with some clients who were using our money to run their business; and some more with 'iffy' clients from whom we were really not sure whether we would recover the money at all. This should be a pointer to you to wisen up quickly. If you are from a business family with a wise accountant or a family business you have inherited, you are lucky; but if you are, like me, a first-generation entrepreneur then you'd better get your act together quickly and take a crash course in finance or read at least 10 books.

Here are some must-read authors just to teach you to love finance.

Rich Dad, Poor Dad by Robert Kiyosaki — this is a classic book. Every post-graduate in management should read this. Of course I would stick my neck out and say every school should have this subject as one of their electives.

Essential Capitalist by Roger Lowenstein

Adventure Capitalist by Jim Rogers

Several more can be recommended, and you can set out discovering your own favourite authors on finance.

Last but not the least: Focus on your clients.

Who are your biggest clients? Do the cash cow quadrant:

You never know when the cash cow will become a laggard and when the laggard who you thought is soon going to the dogs will become a rising star. Keep a close watch on what clients are doing to grow their businesses. After all, in the service industry we are dependent on our

Cash Cow	Rising Stars
Laggards	Dogs

BCG

clients and it is completely in our interest that they are growing and adding new revenue streams. We also need to build our competencies as they are growing so we stay relevant. Else we will become obsolete and they can and will find new partners who are more aligned to their current/future needs. Similarly, keep a watch on clients whose business is going downhill. If it is not in the public domain it is a bit difficult but not impossible. The sales guys are the best bet who can tell you whether there is demand for the product and service, new competition which is coming in etc.

Also, it is very important to focus on your vendors.

This is the reverse of clients. You also need to keep a check on the financial health of your own vendors and also whether they are growing with you. Keep adding new vendors as you are going along — at least two in a year — so you can get different kinds of ideas from them as well. In our organization we are trying to meet this challenge by asking different teams to work on ideas and creatives so people do not slip into a comfort zone.

The comfort zone is the most dangerous as we all know and has been endorsed by many business leaders. It is true to a large extent that only the paranoid survive, thrive and do well. I simply translate this as being proactive, anticipating what could be the changes coming into the industry, internal, external and taking precautionary measures accordingly. Hence an R & D department in every company, not only those in manufacturing or IT, is a must.

An entrepreneur can never take his eye off the ball. He or she has to be continuously focused on what he wants.

What is focus? Where should the focus be? I believe it is like Arjuna seeing only the eye of the bird.

Focus consists of Concentration

On your business, team, delivery, clients, the value you are offering.

Consistency

What you are delivering needs to be consistent. I would take the example of McDonald's. You know what you will get for ₹ 100. A 'happy meal' delivered with the same quality, within an expected time frame in a wrapper with the same uniform taste. There are no surprises here. It is not like a fine dining experience where you expect the chef to perhaps surprise you every time. What you see is what you get. Same with Subway, Natural's ice cream, etc. I often quote that being brilliant but inconsistent is worse than being mediocre but consistent. At best the results may be the same.

Co-operation

You need the co-operation of the team, your key vendors, clients and of course the market place. Contrary to what one reads day in and day out, surprisingly, business is not only about competition. It is also about co-operation. The business is co-dependent with the eco-system: the eco-system you have created should be in synergy. You will read more on that later.

Conclusion

Focus on value, customer satisfaction, customer feedback, trends, forecasting — and of course bottom line. Not to forget vendors, systems / processes, and innovations.

Interview: C. Parthasarathy, Chairman, Karvy Group

Why did you get into the financial sector, and what kept you going?

After I qualified as a Chartered Accountant, it was clear to me that to succeed and grow quickly in life, I had to do something very different. I believed I had the aptitude, because I had done well academically. Also, setting up a traditional CA practice would take a while – first, you have to look for new clients and hope that they grow so that you can grow with them; and then, establishing yourself can take as long as 15 to 20 years. So I got together with some friends who had done their articleship with me in the same CA firm, and we set up Karvy 33 years ago. My parents, both doctors, felt that their only child was taking a big risk in not going for a job – to which my answer was, that was something I could do any time; and they were very supportive.

What was it you did differently?

First, I bought a small computer system from a friend who was working as a management trainee in DCM Sriram. Then I hired a couple of youngsters to create a financial accounting package using Basic and Cobol programming. This was 33 years ago, long before all the software that is so widespread today had been created – even the companies that made them hadn't been set up then! We went out and got clients, who we found hadn't finalized – or even written – their accounts, and offered to do everything for them plus automate their systems. We also got state government bodies like Andhra Pradesh Industrial Development Corporation and other undertakings, finishing their accounts which had not been done for six months, sometimes as long as three years.

There was also something called a 'sensitivity report' which assessing and lending agencies needed for their beneficiaries – we decided that we could do it differently. Within a week, we had hammered out a simple program in Basic which could get these statements out in 15 minutes. We started charging ₹450 per statement, which we raised to ₹750 as the word spread and business picked up. We did a lot of financial statements for big lenders like IDBI, ICICI and IFCI, as well as for borrowers. All this gave us a lot of opportunities to meet many people and gain exposure.

How did you keep building up your business with your specific focus?

Things became difficult after PCs hit the Indian market in 1985 and then Lotus 123 spreadsheets came in. Our USP disappeared overnight – anyone could do what we were doing! But I have the ability to work very hard, and I decided to take my interest in the stock market and make it a business model. Share accounting was an obvious area to look at – so we got into the registrar and share transfer business. TCS was the leader, followed by Datamatics and MAA Services; our difference – and advantage — was that we spoke the same language as the company secretary and CFO, and knew what they wanted beyond mere data processing. We provided it.

We started looking beyond Hyderabad, and saw the entire country as a market – then the whole world. In 1987, we rented a 100-square-foot office in Bombay and tied up with CAs all over India to collect share applications and liaise with the bankers. There was then a technology gap of about 1-1/2 years between the US and India, so we got friends there to send us literature which we could use to upgrade our knowledge. In 1989, when the talk of demutualization and dematerialization of shares began there, we realized that we should also diversify into the registry business.

We got membership of the Hyderabad Stock Exchange in a colleague's name, paying ₹ 50,000 which was the highest at the time. Then SEBI said one must be a full-time employee, so we had to surrender our certificates of practice. In 1991, PRIME rated us the largest IPO registrar because of the number of assignments we got. And when the National Stock Exchange was formed in 1995, we became members immediately. We then joined depositories and the Bombay Stock Exchange, too. By the time the regional exchanges lost their relevance, that didn't affect us as we had already transitioned to the next level.

So I would say that what has kept us ahead is the ability to spot trends ahead of others, which has always given us the first-mover advantage.

Are you keeping that up by getting into new areas still?

Of course! We spun off the registry business as Karvy Computershare, and our full-service stockmarket brokerage as Karvy Stockbroking. We also distribute financial products, which include the top 10 mutual funds. We have 600,000 customers as depository participants, and the same number of broking accounts.

We have also set up another subsidiary, Karvy Commodities Broking, which should be among the top five or six futures brokers, and are members of spot exchanges – these are early days for them, but we use a two-pronged approach: we look at it as both an asset class and a market for people dealing in commodities.

We are also into international commodities including bullion and oil. This is a very exciting area — and profitable to be in but it is in its early stages too.

Case Study: Will-power, tolerance and perseverance

When R.K. Behera set up his business in Jamshedpur nearly 40 years ago, it wasn't easy going. "I struggled for the first six years, and couldn't pay a single paisa to my family," says the Chairman of the nearly ₹2,000-crore RSB group which manufactures a variety of components and systems for the automotive industry. "My brother, who was working for LIC, supported me."

Behera's background was the stuff entrepreneurs are normally made of. He was from a 'very ordinary middle-class family'. His father, who was working for Tata Steel – not in a very high position – borrowed ₹15,000 from his friends to give him his starting capital. Those friends gave the money grudgingly — why couldn't the boy join Bokaro Steel Plant where he was getting a job?

But the young man had, in his own words, 'very strong will-power, tolerance and perseverance'. And he has shown what these qualities can help you achieve in the face of adversity. With no experience of business, his International Auto Products became a sick company in four years, and he couldn't pay back the loans of Bihar State Finance Corporation (BSFC), the bank and the Small Industries Service Institute. Friends continued to advise him to give up. But he wouldn't. The bank gave him a good package, and he found a mentor in A.K. Chowdhury, MD of an Asset Management Company, who fought for Behera and got him an additional loan of ₹ 1 lakh with no security. Following this, BSFC also gave a good package, and Behera was back in business. Eventually, his company became the first in the industrial area to repay BSFC fully.

Sticking to his knitting, Behera – who had now been joined by his brother – managed to get a breakthrough with Tata Motors in 1980 thanks to his quality and customer-centric approach. From then on, there was no looking back: growth hit 80-100 per cent a year till 1995. "We started from a small base, so the percentage is not as great as it sounds," he admits. "But I was earning enough to support my family."

Behera says he could not have achieved what he has without the support of his customers and banks – but the man's personal commitment in the face of all odds obviously counted for much. When he decided to start manufacturing propeller shaft components, for instance, he couldn't afford a consultant's fees; so he prepared the project report on his own. "That helped me to learn finance!" he smiles. And when IDBI once turned down his loan application on the ground that he was not eligible because he already had one unit, he again didn't go to a lawyer or consultant, but studied the eligibility criteria in detail – and found that he was. Burning with fever and 'very disturbed', he faced a major grilling session by 21 interviewers, but emerged triumphant — though with a loan of ₹12 lakhs against the ₹15 lakhs he had asked for.

Even after the Tata Motors relationship began, there were various obstacles. "The challenge was to take their equipment, dismantle and re-install it in our plant, and start production of the prop shafts within 45 days. We took it up, and did it in 25 days!" Behera says. And every time he made a major new investment, a recession hit him immediately. "We kept investing in adverse situations, but came out of the situation every time," he says.

Having faced challenges all through his career, he says only an entrepreneur can face such risks. "You have to believe in yourself. After that, you have to surrender yourself totally to God's will," he adds. "That will let you satisfy all your stake-holders, not just the share-holders."

Get financial literacy

Circa 1998. A young Aziz Poonawalla got a seed loan of ₹ 30,000 from Bharatiya Yuva Shakti Trust (BYST) to set up his own plastic moulding unit in Pune. The BYST-enabled semi-automatic machine allowed him to make larger pieces of as much as 20 grams each, against the earlier two or three grammes. This helped him to graduate from hand-moulded job-work to computer and telephone keys, wristwatch cases and straps, medicine-bottle caps and weighing-scale components for a number of companies, including multinational Philips. Aziz knew how to operate the machine. He knew where to buy his raw material, how to get orders and deliver the products to his customers. But he knew nothing about finance. Till Bharat Nain, an independent consultant and a 'mentor' with BYST, took him in hand.

"He taught me to keep a *chopdi* and write down how much I earned and how much I spent every day. Earlier, I had no idea whether I was making a profit or a loss, I would just take whatever money I got and spend it for whatever was needed: material for the business,

Bharat Nain

groceries for the household..." says Aziz, who went on to win the JRD Tata Quality Award. "Whatever I am, is thanks to my mentor — he taught me to think big, keep detailed accounts, and calculate the cost of my own time." Aziz, who now lives in a large flat in Pune's swanky Kalyani Nagar area, has changed his business model and outsources all the plastic moulding work needed for making the weighing-scale enclosures of which he is now a major specialist supplier to almost everyone who makes scales for the kitchen, laboratory or bathroom. "Even my wife now keeps regular accounts of the household expenses," he says. "We don't budget anything (he obviously doesn't need to!), but we know where the money goes."

Says Bharat himself about his hand-holding of Aziz Poonawalla: "The input-output correlation is very important. *Kitna aaya, kitna gaya?*" An entrepreneur is a very lonely person, he explains: especially because business is a very personal thing – no one in your immediate family and social stratum understands why you are doing what you are doing. That's why the entrepreneur needs a mentor to talk to, who will listen to his ideas – often, a new idea every day so that the mentor has to rein him in and ensure that there is a revenue stream, however small it may be.

So, it is necessary to sense the revenue stream and let it be the bedrock on which to build. That's the base of financial literacy. Something most of us don't understand, he points out, is that land is a dead investment – it doesn't generate any revenue. Once the entrepreneur has learnt all this, he doesn't need the mentor any longer. And the secret of mentorship is to be able to judge when that point comes, when he can withdraw and the entrepreneur can be allowed to fly on his own. "My real success is when he doesn't call me for six months – that proves that he is in his own orbit!" Bharat adds.

The world is full of great businesses which have bitten the dust simply because the entrepreneur has not been financially literate. So what is financial literacy? Is it only reading a balance sheet? No, that is only a good starting point.

By now we have established that we are in business to serve the customer. Right — but what use is it to the customer if you have to shut shop leaving a slew of vendors, employees, consultants and all and sundry unpaid? Business, as I have said elsewhere, is also about profit and loss. At the end of the month unfortunately no amount of philosophy helps. What is required is that everybody needs to be paid including you. So how do you ensure this?

Most entrepreneurs including me are creative people. Left to our own devices we would never look into the book of accounts. Fortunately, early in my life I got introduced to this wonderful book called *Rich Dad, Poor Dad*. I urge everybody to read this book. It opens your mind to the world of creating wealth. I was well into the 8th year of my business before I stumbled on this book. There was no looking back for me after that. I also started attending seminars on Finance, and got interested in investing in the stock market. Now if you are an investor you automatically start reading something about the company in which you have invested. In this way, slowly and steadily, you start researching other companies. This is the best continuing financial education. I also started subscribing to the financial newspapers, several business magazines, and newsletters from equity analysts. There are some very good authors who can be read to improve financial literacy:

Robert Allen	Ram Charan
Donald Trump	Basant Maheshwari
Peter Lynch	Anil Lamba

This improves your world view, not to mention that you will start understanding various nuances of the language spoken across the business world. I am of the opinion that the principles of business are the same across most businesses (I would even stick my neck out to say all businesses, but there may be differences, so let that argument rest).

What is a must in any business is keeping your books meticulously up to date. Record revenue, let bills go out on time and start your collections as soon as your bills have gone.

Keep a collection target every month just like you have a revenue target.

For example:

In the service industry it typically looks like this:

Figures in lakhs

Expenses per month	
Salary	65.0
Consultant fee	5.0
Rent	1.0
Conveyance + Travel	1.0
Communication	1.0
Electricity	0.75
Stationary	0.10
Tea/ coffee	0.10
Employee incentive	1.0
Interest cost	5.0

This is for rule-of- thumb calculation. Please note that employee cost is the highest in a service industry and hence keeping an eye on productivity is a must. Also, continuous re-skilling is a given, as the industry changes at a fast pace - particularly in the digital age.

Collections	upto 31st January 2014	
Business 1		
Client	Expected	Due amount in ₹
ABC	5.2	6.2
XY Z	1.6	1.6
Def	3.2	3.5
Total	10.0	11.3

Bangalore branch		
Client	Expected	Due amount in ₹
ROA	6.4	6.4
PQR	1.4	1.6
Def	3.9	4.5
Total		

Business 2		
Client	Expected	Due amount in ₹
RST	5.2	6.2
123	1.6	1.6
CBA	3.2	3.5
Total		

Other than that, maintain lists of 30, 60, and 90 day creditors and debtors.

Company ABD								
Outstanding statement as on 31st March 2014								
Client	Credit period	< 30 days	30 to 60 days	60 to 90 days	90 -120 days	120 days	Total	Remarks
RAF	30 days	2.5	1.5	1	0.5		5.5	PDC received
XYZ	40 days	3.5		1	0.5		5.0	PDC received

Check what the projected revenue is, and tally it every month with the actual revenue achieved.

Monthly revenue					
Client	Job	Projected Top line	Projected revenue	Achieved Top Line	Achieved revenue
ABC	Print ads	1000000	100000	700000	70000
	Radio ads	200000	20000	300000	30000
TFD	creative	500000	500000	700000	700000
TOTAL		1700000	620000	1700000	800000

Do a month-on-month revenue calculation, and if you deduct expenses, you have your profit or loss month on month. No head of business should wait till the end of the financial year, March, to check whether he is going to make a profit or loss.

The Partha system takes this to a whole new level where they measure profit and loss on a day-to-day basis. It was developed by the Birlas. It is a manual system to determine input costs and the daily cash flows. If you can't do that, the least you can do is to keep track of it on a month-to-month basis without fail. Honestly, this is non-negotiable. I have experimented very successfully with this model of finance, after learning from our own experience of not understanding the real meaning of business in our formative years. We invested in a web technology company a couple of years ago and one of my first pieces of advice to them was: along with an accountant, get a finance guy who will manage finance for you.

By now, we have realized that accounts is different from finance. Accounts is about book-keeping; finance is about business analysis from a financial perspective. I regret to state that M.Com's in India, even if they are rank holders, do not understand finance. There may be exceptions to this — but by and large they do not go beyond a set of antiquated rules studied in an antiquated education system which has no relevance at all from the modern business perspective. Probably a short-term Tally course helps them more than their Master's degree. Sad, but true. So can you leave your finances to your accountant? NO, please! I am of the opinion that finance should be under the eagle eye of the promoter. This is not to say that he or she must be micro-managing but certainly should have access to it every day if required.

Shardul Mohite has been a student entrepreneur, right from the very early days when he was in engineering college. "But back in those days we were just building software and selling website tools to make that extra buck in order to have fun and financial independence," he says. "But fun became passion, which led me to drop out in my final year of engineering to join the UK-based startup Entrap as one of its first employees. That was my first international startup experience, where I learned all the nuances of building a real company, a product, fund raising, hiring etc. But I was not earning any money, as Entrip was a consumer web startup with the ideology of build first and then figure out the revenue model."

After a year or so, Shardul started his own company, Webonise Lab, with a friend. This was in February 2009, when he was only 24 years old. Initially, it was a part service, part product company, but the duo failed to convert their products into a viable business. These included AppBazar, India's first Android marketplace, which would compete directly with Google Play. They then decided to focus on outsourced product development (OPD). "Our own experience and passion for building products helped a lot," Shardul explains. OPD is modeled very much like the IT services business; the only difference is that it takes responsibility for delivery and plays a crucial role in all the decisions related to products and technology."

Till early 2011 Webonise Lab was a profitable business - but it needed to grow threefold in less than year. To tackle this, they made a faulty financial decision: they raised a small investment and put the money "in all the wrong places", Shardul recalls wryly. "But our first investor gave us something more important than money - a retired banker with more professional experience than our combined age was appointed as Financial Adviser/Controller. He changed the way we look at business; he asked tough questions and pushed us to look at places that we never really thought would matter."

A combination of Financial Literacy and Financial Discipline created an environment which was extremely fertile for growth. Shardul personally used both these to empower more people to take decisions and spend money at the right place to make more money. This decentralization of financial authority helped move things faster, the vendors loved them as they were paid on - or sometimes even before - time, and the customer also paid on time. At one time, webonise lab was sitting on 55% EBIDTA - which they decided was too high. At the next board meeting, the directors decided to bring down the EBIDTA by increasing employee compensation and investing in long-term goals. "I would say Financial Literacy and Financial Discipline both played significant roles in the 300% YOY growth of Webonise after 2011," he adds. And then comes the revelation: The investor was none other than Kiran Bhat!

In early 2013, Webonise was acquired by a US-based sports marketing company, and Shardul started looking for what to do next. After months of research and ideation, he came across a 'massive opportunity' in DIY HD (do-it-yourself high-definition) video making, using smartphones. Thus was born YogurtLabs, of which he is CEO. "Yougurt is going to be a platform for providing tools and a marketplace for this kind of short videos," says. "Primarily, we are starting with SMEs that are continuously looking to make videos for their social media communities. But once the technology is ready, it will be used to create multiple apps on multiple platforms with more consumer focus uses, like birthday videos, travel films, videos for parties and other events. Another way to look at what we are doing is: a new-age tech-enabled video production house which is run as a platform that will make more commercial and personal videos in the next two years than any video production house has made in a decade!"

Keep an eye on expenses. This is common advice. However what I am saying is keep an eye on the quality of the expenses. Let me give you an example.

You have increased your expenses by say 25 percent? What is it for? Is it going to give you proportionate revenue in a couple of months, one year? If for a period of 6 months you are going to lose money then maybe you should start calculating the quality of revenue. What kind of revenue is it for which you have increased expenses? If you are projecting a windfall and you are okay with the loss for a whole year because the yield after one year will be better than your current revenue streams, then you are fine.

Example of some revenue vs expense sheets:

TABLE 1 - Regular Revenue Stream - In lakhs

Expense		Revenue	
Heads	Amount	Heads	Amount
Manpower	65	Media	Aaa
Conveyance	5	Creative	Vvv
Electricity	5	XXX	Bbb
Travel	15	YYY	
Interest	10		
TOTAL	100		150

TABLE 2 - Increased Expenses Reflected in the Revenue Stream - In lakhs

Expense		Revenue	
Heads	Amount	Heads	Amount
Manpower	80	Media	Aaa
Conveyance	10	Creative	Vvv
Electricity	7	XXX	Bbb
Travel	20	YYY	
Interest	20		
TOTAL	137		170

In this table the expense has increased by 37 percent and the revenue by about 13 percent. This is fine provided you know that there is future revenue going to be generated due to increase in expenses.

TABLE 3 - Increased Expense vs Revenue- In lakhs

Please do an analysis of this chart. Check the revenue vs expenses compared to the first chart

Your revenue component is roughly 40 percent vs 50 percent in Table 1. So even if you have increased expenses your revenue as compared to Table 1 has reduced. So you check for yourself whether additional expansion has really benefited the company.

Expense		Revenue	
Heads	Amount	Heads	Amount
Manpower	90	Media	Aaa
Conveyance	10	Creative	Vvv
Electricity	8	XXX	Bbb
Tr avel	25	YYY	
Interest	25		
TOTAL	158		220

This is what we need to check. Example: in Table 2, expenses are increased by 37 percent and revenue increment has only been 13 percent (approx.). However, from Table 1 too, expenses have increased by more than 50 percent and revenue too has gone up by 50 percent (approx.).

So what have you really achieved?

However, this is fine as long as you know there is incremental revenue coming from some new revenue streams in the coming years with marginal increase in expense.

Disclaimer: This is just one way to analyse income versus expenses. The above is relevant for mature businesses and not necessarily for start-ups.

Increase in expense

You can now check if for the same revenue stream you have increased your expenses, say by 50 percent, and your return is still going to be, say, 15 percent. Then you are potentially in the danger zone.

However if the expenses are for a new revenue stream where you are expecting a yield of, say, 30 percent and you have a solid plan ahead of you, then it may be worth your while pursuing the thought process.

What I am trying to say here is that continuous analysis of what you are doing is a must. The danger zone for an entrepreneur is when they have achieved some modicum of success and then put up a new line just for kicks, for an ego massage or worse, without a revenue stream or thinking it through.

Several people got into the airline business perhaps only for the glamour value or some other hidden benefits. Similarly the satellite TV business is also strewn with several such failures. The Business India group, for example, went into television as early as in 1989, when channels could not uplink from India – BiTV had to be beamed from Nepal. And it didn't get a decent transponder, so it had to use a Russian satellite for which its sales force had to canvass support from cable TV operators and persuade them to install an additional dish to receive its signals.

Ashok H. Advani, a barrister at law from London who promoted the Group, is definitely not financially illiterate – his first venture *Business India*, which he launched in February 1978 as the first magazine reporting on the Indian corporate world, was a runaway success. So was *Inside Outside*, which continues to be what it claims: India's most respected and highest circulated interior design magazine. But Business India Television International, which was projected to have five separate channels and would bring in the country's first outdoor broadcasting vans (OBVs), proved to be a drain on the Group's resources. Good money followed bad, and Ashok went on sinking money into the project: his own, then funds borrowed across a spectrum of friends in industry and business, his employees' dues – salaries and benefits have not been paid even to those who lost their jobs when BiTV closed down in the mid 1990s, while the magazines' staff salaries are in arrears of a year and more.

One year, he was even arrested by the Economic Offences Wing and had to post bail to be at the Taj Hotel to receive guests at *Business India's* premier event, the 'Businessman of the Year' award function. So what happened? The success of one venture after another obviously blinded the promoter to the possibility of failure; and a series of 'advisers' added to the problem. A first-rate accountant may have helped, if his sane advice had been heeded.

Retail opened up, especially EBOs (exclusive business outlets), sometime in early 2000, and it has ended in bankruptcy for several companies. It has spared no retailer, be it in children's apparel or women's apparel or sleepwear companies. The biggest names in retail took on too much debt, expanded like crazy and finally could not grow as fast as they had predicted or projected in their business plans.

I would not go so far as to say that these companies, some of which actually contribute to the GDP of the country, do not have financial literacy. All I am saying is that keeping your eye on finance at all times is a must. Several old-timers have accountants whom they inherited along with the family business, who know how to keep books as per traditional business community practice.

Maybe it is time for Management colleges to study our ancient business bookkeeping practices and introduce these into the curriculum.

All budding businessmen can benefit immensely from attending programs like finance for non-finance people. This can really help you navigate through basic terminology, apart from guiding your accounts department to increase efficiency and productivity.

I know clients who despite having a wonderful product went bust only because they did not keep an eye on Finance. Here I would like to say that it is best to hand-pick your team — finance, accounts, legal - and work with the best minds you can get. One of India's sleepwear manufacturers spent a lot of time and energy — and sleepless nights — paying attention to the brand, the photography, the look and feel for his advertisements; but alas, no attention was being paid to revenues, month-on-month collection, or profitability of stores on a standalone basis.

A lot of what I have written here looks elementary but you see that if it is not practised then you are defeating the very purpose of your business.

The three mantras of a successful brand or business, according to Kishor Chhabria, CEO of Blue Bells Inc, are vision, hard work and seed capital. He had all three in 2002 when he launched his Sleep-ins brand of sleepwear for women. Over the next seven years, he painstakingly built up a top line of ₹ 150 crore. Sleep-ins gained a reputation for integrating contemporary design with precision and quality, a network of 30 company-owned stores and a presence in 300 multi-brand outlets across 25 cities.

Even when Kishor's seed capital was invested and spent, angel investors were willing to bet on him and his story, and finance kept flowing in year on year. So money, in his view, does not play a very important part in growing a brand. One thing he would like to tell the world, however, is: "Spending is in our hands - so spend wisely. Creating a brand is no child's play, you need to cross oceans, deserts and forests before you start climbing the mountains."

All that came to a brutal end when a devastating fire in 2009 ruined everything. Kishor just went out of business. He lost wealth in millions and had to face criminal actions and 'all sorts of issues from various fronts'. It took nearly four years for the storm to settle – but in the second half of 2013, he decided to take a U-turn to repeat history and restore the brand's lost glory. "It took me 15 years to create India's largest and most recognisable nightwear brand. This time, I shall turn it around in less than five years with limited resources with my fighting attitude and an intact vision," he says, adding: "The real test of a winner is…. How many times can you bounce back from failure?"

Many a time, says Naresh Sareen, Managing Director of white goods retailer Dass Electric Trading Co. Pvt. Ltd, a businessman relies on his C.A for advice on financial matters. This may be right or wrong –

but financial literacy is a must to make any business a success. This alone helps you to decide at what price a product should be purchased, what overheads will go in determining the lowest selling price and at what volume. The focus on planning leads seamlessly to cost based thinking and cost should be in the control of the entrepreneur. For the largest part of the cost, he or she should play the role of a customer to decide how many employees to hire, how many square feet of real estate to lease, how much to spend on advertising and so on; and, like the customer who has limitations of budget, should at time stop buying a particular good or service to keep the financials in control.

It is simple to know that revenue planning is difficult because customers and market scenario are in charge of this, but planning costs is in your hands, Naresh says. To get finances from banking institutions at a very high and fixed rate of interest increases your risk and fixed cost.

Quoting Mike Tyson's "Everyone has a plan until they get punched in the mouth" and the example of Napoleon who ended up first on the island of Elba and eventually in the grave despite his brilliance, Naresh warns that this can be the fate even for the most successful of strategists.

Narayan Rajan, CEO of i-Vista Digital Solutions Pvt Ltd which he founded in Bangalore in 1996 at the age of 21, says an entrepreneur's personal perspective depends on the life cycle of his or business. In the beginning, it is important to get customers and deliver to the customer. Financial literacy is less important, as it can be left to a C.A. or a financial consultant. Narayan always believed that he himself didn't need to know what a balance sheet looked like – but that, he admits in retrospect, was 'a big mistake'.

When his business – which "ideates and creates tailored marketing solutions that break the monotony of digital creative marketing" - was just two years old, it got its first bank facility. Narayan had to look at things that he had no idea about – financial ratios! So he just took a consultant along, and everything fell in place. But the following year, and again a year later, he had to go in for fresh financing and faced the same questions again. "I was blank! I decided that I couldn't stay in a state of ignorance," he says. "So I decided to get a grip on these mysterious ratios. I still don't understand everything, but I'm much better today."

Believing strongly that an entrepreneur needs more and more financial literacy as he or she goes on, he looked at other companies' balance sheets in the US, and learnt how much more insight the GAAP gives. "But I still rate the customer much, much higher than finance," he adds.

A checklist:

- Monthly billing to be sent on time to customers

- Get vendor bills on time

- Check salaries and other expenses. Keep a list handy

- What are the other expenses?

- Check for statutory compliances like Service Tax, VAT, TDS

- Maintain a monthly revenue chart

- Maintain an expense chart

- Show PBT calculation

- Check cash flow: are bills going on time? Are receivables coming in on time?

- Check the 30/60/90 days sheet

- Is mid-term/long-term finance in place? Cash credit limits, overdraft facilities, bank application, guarantees

- Check revenue and expense statements regularly. Ask for projection at the beginning of the month and check what has been achieved at the end of the month

What we are saying here is: keeping an eye on the incoming and outgoing is as important as continuously keeping an eye on product quality, innovations, customer service, etc.

Take a line of credit before you need it. There is a saying that bankers lend money only to those who don't need it. The needier you are, the more difficult it will be to raise money. So when everything is going fine and you don't really need the money, that particular time in your business when you are recording 30 percent YOY revenue improvement, take a line of credit. Don't use it if you don't want to. But let it be there.

The dynamics of business may change. There was a time when our TDS component was manageable, but three years ago we changed our business model to going a little slow in media and concentrating more on design. Soon our revenue changed from 20:80 (20 creative and 80 media) to 50:50.

So where was the catch? In media we got 60 days' credit, but in retainers- which were pertaining to salaries- we had to pay immediately, even though money coming in from the client took 60 to 100 days. Plus, our TDS for this was 10 percent. So in the last three years we have been reeling under cash-flow issues due to this one single anomaly which we did not foresee when we made the change in the strategy. Realization of the nature of the problem is one big step in trying to correct a situation.

Business is like a permanent jigsaw puzzle; and if it does not seem like one to you then you and your business may be stagnating. You are not learning anything new and you are not solving enough puzzles!

Finance is also about developing an innovative mind. You need to see patterns. Remember, pattern recognition is a part of the mind games we played as children. Pattern recognition activities require children to observe and continue patterns preparing them for learning to recognize numbers. This is actively taught in schools.

This is exactly what is required in business. Well, practise it now. Also learn how to handle complexities. Remember that your earning power is directly proportionate to how many complex challenges you can solve — not only for your company but, most importantly, for your clients.

For example, if you study the revenue sheets you will notice at a very elementary level that your numbers may look good for Q3 and Q4. From the revenue for the last couple of years, a pattern is bound to emerge depending on your industry and the kind of work you do. However, in most business there are fixed overheads even for quarters in which you don't have revenue. In sectors like agriculture, too, there is no consistent revenue for all the 12 months. Hence the farmer has to rotate his crops and may have some other ancillary crops like pepper, bananas or chilies along with his main revenue stream of wheat, rice or sugarcane. You can also figure out your pricing based on the seasonality of your business.

So don't wait. Sign up today for a basic financial literacy class and learn how to read a balance sheet, what is cash flow, what is leverage, what is net worth, what are fixed assets, what is expense. Happy learning!

Interview: Dr Anil Lamba, Founder & Director, Lamcon School of Management

How important is financial literacy?

Financial literacy is the most important attribute for any businessperson. If there are five important ingredients necessary for business, and you have four but you are financially illiterate, you will get into serious trouble. In fact, financial illiteracy is guaranteed to kill your business. It is a total myth that profit is the result of your ability to make and sell alone. If that were true, how do you explain why two people making and selling the same product do not do equally well? Take an example from the mid-1980s, when a new textile tycoon who was a genius in financial management suddenly erupted on the scene. Were his (or his people's) weaving skills superior to those of the company that was ruling the market till then? No. He prospered, and beat his rival, because his financial management skills were far superior.

Most business failures in the world have been because of bad financial management. Some estimates say that this is solely responsible for the demise of nine out of every 10 failed businesses. And this applies even to countries and economies – look at the recent US sub-prime crisis, and those crises that continue to affect European countries like Greece, Portugal and Spain. Whether it is a corporate or a country, good financial management is a must.

So are you saying that a businessman who doesn't have finance skills is doomed to failure?

These skills were inborn in the businessman I've mentioned – but even if you don't have them, you can acquire them. There is no getting away from the fact that financial know-how is the most important ingredient for success. You as an entrepreneur should have it – you can't just delegate it. Earlier, the engineers ruled the roast: those who knew how to make a product; then it was the day of the marketer who knew how to sell the product. In the 1990s, finance came into its own.

Why does the entrepreneur or businessman need to acquire financial literacy? Surely he can just hire good finance people?

That's myth no. 2: that financial management happens only in the finance department. What happens there is only accounting. Every individual in the organization must have the ability to understand the impact of his or her every action on the bottom line. The basic thumb rule is that what you earn must be more than, or at least equal to, your cost; but the perception of cost is itself usually wrong. Take an example: if you are running an airline, and you need to fill aviation fuel worth ₹ 10 lakh for a particular flight. Now, if your capacity is 200 passengers, your cost per seat is ₹ 5,000 plus, say, ₹ 200 for passenger amenities like water and, maybe, a sandwich and tea or coffee. You fix the ticket price at ₹ 9,000. Now suppose you have a flight ready to take off with only 80 passengers, and someone comes rushing up at the last minute and says he wants a seat but can afford to pay only ₹ 1,500. What do you do?

You must take him on – because even that fraction of your regular ticket price is an additional income that cuts your cost. And this is a decision that needs to be taken by the people manning the front office, or ticket counter – they need to be empowered to take the call. That's what makes the difference between survival and failure. Making profits actually makes the businessperson complacent – he or she becomes blind to the many wrong financial decisions being taken down the line. Financial management has to become a culture across the organization – like the simple notice on the inside of a conference room asking the last person who leaves to switch off the lights. That in itself may be a negligible saving, but – you know the proverb about little drops of water!

Actually, financial management is practised all the time across the organization, and it can cause problems even if you have a strong finance department. When a salesman in the field bargains on prices or agrees to a buyer's demand for an extended credit period for a potentially large order, he is involved in financial management. A shop floor supervisor deciding on the amount of inventory needed, or a production schedule, is making a financial decision. So is the person who decides on the 'bench' size in an information technology company, for potential recruits to wait in the wings. And every one of them must be good at financial management, not just a handful of people in the formal finance function.

So do you offer entrepreneurs something like a mantra for financial discipline?

There are, essentially, two rules. One, you must recognize that no money is free: you have to consider not only the cost of production, but also the cost of the capital. Understand the cost of money, and ensure that you invest only where you can earn as much or more than that cost. The biggest misconception is that the business owner's money is free: it is not!

Rule no. 2 is that the money raised by, or invested in, a business is not a gift. Just look at any company's balance sheet, and you will see that capital is listed as a 'liability'. Ergo, it has to be paid back - so you must be very clear about the inflow from any investment before the outflow happens, and invest it accordingly. Your assets must earn you money all the time.

Both these rules are sacred. Violating either one of them will inevitably lead to the failure of the business. If you analyze the reasons behind any failure, you will find that either or both of these rules has been violated. Look at the big failures of our time, from the Subhiksha retail chain which had been set up by a gold medallist from an IIM, to Kingfisher Airlines and, most recently, SpiceJet. The problem with the airlines has been that they were using short-term money for long-term purposes – selling discounted tickets for far in the future and using that revenue to meet their operating expenses. So when the far-off future became the present, they didn't have the money in hand. The right money must always go to the right place!

Case Study: Lessons of Liberalisation

Hemant Kanoria, Chairman and Managing Director, Srei

Srei Infrastructure Finance is a pioneer in infrastructure financing in India. In over 22 years of operation, Srei has empowered more than 30,000 entrepreneurs through its bouquet of services in the infrastructure sector.

There was never a dearth of entrepreneurial talent in India. The economic liberalisation that the government of India embraced in 1991 has only unshackled the spirit of entrepreneurism. Post-liberalisation, Indian industry has matured a lot. India Inc. has not only competed with its global peers in the Indian market, but also made its presence felt outside India. Today, India is not only a recipient in terms of foreign investment, there is also substantial outflow of FDI from India every year.

As agriculture is a principal occupation for a vast majority in India, rural India always plays an important role in any economic change. Liberalisation does have an impact on rural India, but the extent is yet to be realised fully. Substantial public finance has been channeled into schemes aimed at developing rural India. This has translated into higher per capita income and literacy rate in rural India. But the improvements have only been in patches and in a scattered manner.

[**SOWse:** B*oar in Boots – A Business Travelogue* by Parthasarathi Swami (Fortytwo Bookz Galaxy, 2012)]

After 33 years in business, Kanoria talks of what it takes to update and upgrade oneself from a kirana shop to a ₹ 50,000-crore infrastructure financing business. Challenges and opportunities are entwined - every challenge is an opportunity, he believes. "You should get a kick out of facing challenges, but you also get kicked; you should get a kick out of that, too!" Hemant Kanoria says. Every entrepreneur should be able to open the box of challenges and look at the opportunities one by one – then sit back regularly and ask himself or herself whether the model is institutionalized and replicable. Different people have different aims and expectations: creating wealth, creating an institution to live on after themselves...

For Hemant, the challenge that caught his attention was infrastructure. "It was a problem. I had this fanciful imagination that I should do something for the country. So when I saw an opportunity, I got into it – with 16 hours of load-shedding every day, I really didn't know what I was getting into!" he says. "But it has been the most interesting journey, I have enjoyed it thoroughly. There have been lots of challenges, but we managed to steer through all of them successfully with ongoing review and innovation. When you are in a corner, you have only one way to go: upwards. So you must scale the wall – like Spiderman."

The big thing in a business that is so totally centred around finance is TRUST, which needs to be 100 percent. Srei has a zero-tolerance policy on integrity. Punishment is harsh when integrity is compromised. People who fall foul are fired within 15 minutes flat, without worrying about the consequences. On the other hand, people know that there is no 'hire-and-fire' policy, so they won't be thrown off if the ship is in a storm. And despite being a financial institution in a place like Kolkata, they work 24x7 when necessary, landing up in office even on 'Bandh' days.

Add a new revenue stream every year

Start an incubation unit and then scale it up. Anand Mahindra famously said that his company is in a marathon and not a sprint race. The context changes when you think like that. A sprint runner has a different mindset. He would like to milk the market and his customer quickly and maybe get into something else after that. I have no quibbles with a businessman who does that. But there is merit in running a marathon. A marathon runner has to have more stamina as he has to run that 42+ km vs a sprinter who probably exhausts himself after the 100-metre dash. When you think of your business like an exciting never-ending marathon, your thinking and mindset as an entrepreneur will be totally different.

You will treat your team, various revenue streams /business from a long-term perspective. You will know that same revenue stream may not throw up cash in years to come.

The key is to keep checking which revenue stream is at what stage of the cycle. Of course, before that it is a good idea to see which revenue streams you have and the expense vs revenue against that. Where are your best resources being allocated? Surprise, surprise! Your best resources may not necessarily be in the cash-cow revenue stream. They may be in the rising star quadrant. What is important is to be aware of who is where. Many traditional businesses may not even be aware about the various revenue streams and may not be plotting them so scientifically.

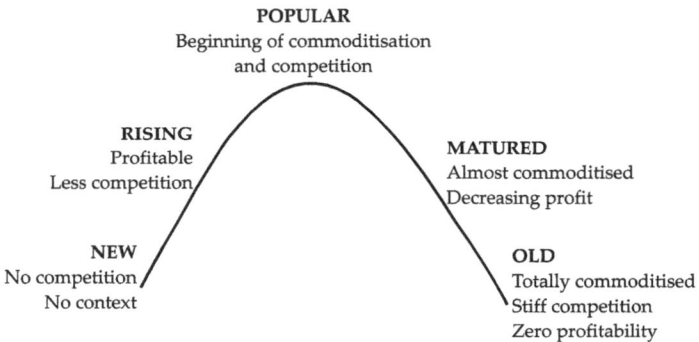

POPULAR
Beginning of commoditisation
and competition

RISING
Profitable
Less competition

MATURED
Almost commoditised
Decreasing profit

NEW
No competition
No context

OLD
Totally commoditised
Stiff competition
Zero profitability

Why do you need to add a revenue stream every two years? Why should you not be perfectly happy with the revenue stream you already have? Let's take the example of an Udupi restaurant. In earlier days they were faithful to their roots and served the traditional fare like idli, dosa etc. Gradually, they started adding Punjabi dishes. Today if you check an Udupi restaurant menu it will offer Mexican, Chinese, Jain, Gujarati and what not. What is the pressure for the restaurateur to do that? When families visit, each member wants to eat a different thing. The children will want pizza, the parents Punjabi and the grandmother may want dosa. He is catering to his customers with multiple cuisines. The regular middle-class family does not visit speciality restaurants. They would rather go to a moderately priced multi-cuisine restaurant and keep the entire family happy.

Now what would have happened to the Udupi if he had not added those new revenue streams? He would have become extinct sooner or later, or his definition would have been very narrow for breakfast and probably high tea. He would have missed out on the huge opportunity of lunch and dinner. Not to mention the fact that he can charge higher prices for the Mexican, Chinese and Pizza. So now he has not only increased his revenue streams to add higher value items, but also kept his overall price moderate as compared to speciality restaurants.

Similarly a branding design house can add multiple new revenue streams like Digital, pure Design, Brand consultancy... branch out further into Trade Fair design, and so on. In other words, offer more services in the same sphere of communications.

As an entrepreneur, you need to recognize where your best resources are or where you need to place them. It is a strategic call: should your young star be put in charge of turning around a dying revenue stream, or should he be in an upcoming one? Should you kill it completely, what will be the repercussions? These are questions an entrepreneur needs to keep asking himself. What should die and what should thrive? What should be under observation? Not to forget how government policies affect a lot of businesses. The minute the government knows an industry is making money, you can be assured that new taxes will be introduced. So how to make money and protect your margin?

The jury is out on diversifying beyond one's core competency. I would say that you should incubate a new project only if you can devote at least one hour a day to it. Optionally, find the brightest kids in the company and make them incubate the new revenue stream or business.

Adding a new revenue stream at least once every two years is now no longer what you need to contemplate longer — one has to simply do it. It keeps the team and promoters on their toes and prevents a business growing old.

Any business today has to keep reinventing itself in order to be relevant. Let's look at a multiplex. People are no longer satisfied with only a soft drink-popcorn combo. They want to be pampered. Enter full recliners with thin-crust pizza and wine or beer to choose from. Keep changing the product mix. Surprise the customer. Similarly a mall also has to keep adding new revenue streams right from flea markets to gourmet food courts. After all, we as customers are very fickle and will change a service provider fairly quickly, as we are flooded with choice.

A new revenue stream also helps from a strategic perspective. Many times we need to keep competition at bay. A particular revenue stream may not be making money but if a competitor offers it, it can create an easy entry into a coveted client's business and soon the competition may be picking up business for other things as well. So you may have to add a revenue stream just to maintain the entry barrier. Every business would only like to cater to that stream which makes money. But a customer most of the time wants convenience and likes to buy a lot of the stuff from the same source. Every service or product does not make money but a service provider or a store has to provide it so that the customer continues to buy the other higher value stuff also from him. He may have to subsidise some service to keep a client happy

But by and large adding a revenue stream keeps a business young, adds value to existing customers, opens doors to new markets and customers, and helps you attract a different kind of manpower which hitherto did not exist in your business. Honestly if you ask me it is a no-brainer.

Also, it is a strategy for risk mitigation. Like we discussed earlier in the chapter, the cash cows may become laggards and the dogs may become extinct. So then what happens to your company? Look at Kodak. They were pioneers in film but they just could not get their digitization act together. What if they had incubated digital technology for photography/cameras? Sure, it may have cannibalized their existing business — but that would have become extinct anyway! I would stick my neck out to say the same about Nokia. They missed the touch revolution and dual SIM to which youngsters had taken a fancy, by at least two years. By the time they woke up and smelt the coffee, nimble-footed competitors had taken over. What if they had incubated this new revenue stream before the market matured?

Two industries, with manufacturing facilities almost cheek by jowl in the Gurgaon industrial area, have approached this differently. While Sandhar Technologies has gone in for a wide variety of new products every few years, Rico Auto Industries has stuck to its core competence but kept widening its geographic reach. One of the reasons Jayant Davar, vice chairman and MD of Sandhar, got into entrepreneurship was what we have described earlier as wrong reason #1: to make 'pots of money'. But, he adds, "I was also keenly interested in engineering, creating value by manufacturing something."

Having decided to 'look at things on my own' and rejected an MBA scholarship offer, young Jayant borrowed ₹ 30,000 from his father – who was reluctant but told him to 'take it and jump'. During 28 years of navigating a path which had its ups and downs but gave him 'a sense of gratification' at every new step, Jayant found that things 'just happened, with no particular method'. Beginning with sheet metal stamping, he soon got bored with this and moved into automotive locks. "I kept picking up anything as a challenge," he says. "That gives you better gratification." He made Sandhar into the largest producer in Asia, making 65,000 sets a day; but in 1991-92, he got bored with locks and moved into mirrors. Continuing to get into new businesses where, as he points out, "one has nothing to do with the other", he got into a joint venture for car door handles, then bought a company making wheels and one making tractor cabins, and set up one to make back panels for television sets.

"I acquired a company in Spain which made plastics and aluminium castings. I didn't know the business, but it excited me," he explains. "Entrepreneurship is like being a child in a candy store. My passion keeps me going!" Sandhar is now a ₹ 1,500-plus crore company with some 6,000 people in 27 manufacturing plants in India and abroad – a long journey for a company that started with a miniscule capital and 12 people.

Rico Auto Industries began earlier, in the late 1970s, but is about the same size, having reported consolidated revenues of ₹ 1,500 crore in 2012-13 and an employee count of 5,200 in 15 plants. Arvind Kapur, MD, also began small – with a family business making sewing machines in Ludhiana. "I was very ambitious, and had a strong desire to set up on my own," he recalls. "So I just plunged into it."

Another common factor he shares with Sandhar is the connection with Industrial Finance Corporation of India: while Jayant's father D.N. Davar, now chairman of the group, had retired from IFCI, Arvind got a lot of encouragement and financial assistance from it. He too kept adding new revenue streams – but unlike Jayant, who always moved into unrelated areas, he stuck to precision components in iron and aluminium for automotive engines and transmission systems. "I started with two-wheeler parts, and moved progressively to cars, trucks and off-road vehicles," he explains. He also moved up the value chain in his products, but stuck to his knitting – he hasn't gone beyond auto components. Rico now manufactures clutch components and oil pump assemblies too. Arvind always had his eyes on foreign markets, and believes that the 'real market' is overseas: "It's 98 percent of the overall market, and we've always looked at that." In 1988-89, he began exporting to Japan, then to the US. "Most American companies were looking at cheaper sourcing, and we managed to become the first to start delivering."

Wisdom, I have realized, is always hindsight. So why not change the rules of the game by having some foresight to incubate some new revenue streams? Let me add that some revenue streams you have thought of may be too premature. I recently heard that Apple had the iPad ready for rollout before the iPhone but Steve Jobs realized that the market was not ready for it. They would not have a context for it. Once the users were used to the iPhone, the iPad was almost a natural extension. I thought that was a brilliant example of consumer insight.

At Demag, Germany, the world leader in industrial cranes which has supplied more than 600,000 cranes in its 195-year history, more than 30 per cent of its global revenue comes from the services business. This is partly because of the very large population of old cranes that need maintenance and upgrade support, and also because this area is the most profitable and steady as it is not prone to industrial cycles.

In India, however, Demag is only 15 years old – so there are fewer of their cranes installed, limiting the revenue in 2006 to under 5 per cent of the company's country revenue – mainly from services that could be provided to non- Demag cranes. Suhas Baxi, who was at that time heading the company's operation in Pune, got an idea: with industrial cranes in India dating back to the 1950s and having been imported from Eastern Europe or built locally with the old European technology, most technological advances had not come in. So, he thought, why not a 'Crane Life Extension Programme'? This would use the heavy old structures and add new technology to provide superior performance, longer life and a lower running cost. "It's a little bit like putting a Volkswagen engine, controls and drive experience in an Ambassador body," explains Suhas, former CEO at the Hyderabad-based Pennar Industries.

The execution needed concept selling, consulting, engineering and project management as local competencies. Demag India created a separate team to focus on the 30,000-plus old cranes in the market. Pilot projects were carefully selected and implemented. The result: a success story, which has formed the basis of a new revenue line.

Demag has been able to grow the services business in India to a level of 20 per cent of its revenue, and growing every year independent of the industrial growth situation. The crane life extension team in India is also a base to provide back-office services on engineering to other Demag companies around the world.

For a car manufacturer who does 'C' segment cars, SUVs or MUVs could be a natural new revenue stream. Who knows, maybe accessories too could add value - like a tablet holder, Bluetooth or whatever the modern professional needs to be connected to his home and office.

For a sports goods retailer what could be the new revenue streams? Could be community play areas where he can tie up with property developers and he could run the entire show with help of coaches etc with whom he would already have a relationship as they buy wholesale from his store.

For a toy manufacturer it could be having events with high tea for children where they get to touch and feel the toys and meet other children. His revenue would automatically increase as the likelihood of children buying after the event is very high.

Lakme has added salons as a wonderful new revenue stream. So has the less known Calvin Klein in Chennai. They have multiple advantages with this one.

    a.   Direct interaction with customers which every company would love to have

    b.   Usage of all their salon products

    c.   Demo of new products

    d.   Brand proliferation: every signage will act as a billboard

    e.   Women become brand ambassadors automatically as word of mouth for salons is very high

You can think of many more.

A farsan manufacturer keeps on adding to his revenue stream, so do the large soft drink companies. Any well-run company thinks of new revenue streams. Whether you want to introduce one in six months or two years depends on your capability to manage a new stream, the resources you can put behind it, your own mindset and enthusiasm to do it. There is no hard-and-fast rule. As long as you can manage the change, the supply chain, the team and the cash you are the best judge of how often you can do it. In our company we have decided once in two years is good, as right now it takes that much time for a stream to become self-sufficient.

An exercise to help you evaluate revenue streams:

What are the revenue streams you currently have?

How much does each contribute to top line and bottom line?

What is the resource allocation against each?

What is the quality of the resource allocation?

What are the expenses against the income?

Can you put your revenue stream in the quadrant? You can make your own quadrant as you go along.

Now think which revenue stream can go extinct and which can be a potential cash cow, and what else you need to keep in your new revenue pipeline.

Interview: Vikram S. Kirloskar, vice chairman, Toyota Kirloskar Motor

You took the Kirloskar Group beyond its traditional strengths of water pumps and oil engines, into high-tech automotives with Japanese collaboration. What drew you?

We have always been an engineering group. And don't forget, my grandfather S.L. Kirloskar was manufacturing engines anyway. When I came back from college, everything was in quite a mess. I decided that the automotive industry would be the locomotive of growth, so I chased it.

Also, the Kirloskars are no strangers to the Japanese: we have had collaborations with them for decades, including Ibara which is still running very successfully, and with Toyoda Textile Machinery, which we brought in long before we set up Toyota Kirloskar Motor in 1997. My wife Geetanjali has also been chairperson of the India-Japan Initiative for a long time. TKM has been in the forefront of the Indian automotive industry almost since it came into the market with the Qualis which was a runaway success.

Anyway, during the industrialisation and development of a country one often ends up coming up with products, goods or services before there is a requirement or commercial demand. So timing is very important – if you take too long, you lose out. We had come out with Kirloskar Tractors of 40-60 horsepower when the economic growth was only 2 per cent and the market was for 20hp. The product was way ahead of its time.

With Toyota, the timing was just right. The product was the right one, at the right time. I can take credit for pushing for the Qualis to start with instead of a car model. And I've learnt a lot from Toyota.

My forte has always been building factories, which is not necessarily entrepreneurial. Yes, one or two had to be closed down, but these closures too gave so much hindsight on what not to do the next time. Net, I've added many factories to the Group.

Are you doing anything else with the Japanese?

That is really exciting. Again, it is Geetanjali's initiative more than mine – she conceived of the vision. We are setting up a chain of state-of-the-art hospitals with Japanese collaboration in a 50:50 partnership with Secon and Susho, the trading arm of the Toyota group. The first is nearing completion. It's a complete family project: our daughter Manasi, who has got her Bachelor of Fine Arts degree from the US, is working on it hands-on, 24x7. She has been running around Bangalore selecting tiles and paint, and talking to the architects and builders to ensure that everything is just right – functionally and aesthetically.

We are doing everything from design to product management. The partnership came about because of our experience of working with the Japanese, and the fact that we have friends in Japan.

Will these be corporate hospitals?

Yes, obviously they must earn a profit. We had decided to set them up not for a return on investment, but they need to make enough money to run themselves. As we got into the project, we realized that we have to run it as a business, or it can't grow. But there is no immediate expectation, only a vision. God knows when we'll get a return. Our hospitals will be run on totally professional lines, with quality and other systems in place that our experience in industry will help us to implement. We'll implement many things we have learnt from operations management in our factories: logistics, material and people flow, and documentation of the processes. We have looked at various things that most other hospitals don't have - for example, there are separate sets of lifts for patients and the service staff so that there is no infection through contamination with, say dirty plates or used linen. Visitors too will have earmarked facilities. We are also doing a lot on fire safety: for example, the kitchen is not in the basement.

The financial arrangements will ensure that we have enough equity and less debt – we don't want to over-leverage borrowings. As much as ₹ 130 crore of the project cost of ₹ 200 crore will be equity. Once this takes off, we want to build several hospitals to provide quality healthcare.

Case Study: Sticking to the knitting

Dilip Shanghvi, managing director of Sun Pharmaceutical Industries, has always been clear that on one front he could never compete with the late Steve Jobs of Apple. "Jobs employs only the best," he says. "We can't be so selective. We employ ordinary people and get the best out of them."

What makes Sun special? It's a speciality drug company concentrating on areas like cardiology, psychiatry, neurology, diabetology, ophthalmology and orthopaedics. It is the market leader in speciality therapy areas in India and the fifth largest pharma company by prescription sales. It has a presence in more than 40 other countries. With a 2011-12 turnover of ₹ 8,000 crore ($1.45 billion), Sun is a minnow by global standards. But Shanghvi prefers to stay that way. "If you look at the pharma industry, most of the wealth is created by small companies," he says.

The Sun story – a first generation entrepreneurial success – is about sticking to the knitting or backward integration, depending on how you see it. Shanghvi's father was a trader in Kolkata in the medicines his son would later make. He graduated in commerce – "medicine seemed too difficult" - and joined his father. The real challenge, he realised, lay in manufacture, not trade. So he moved to Gujarat – closer to the markets and distribution channels – and set up his first factory. The rest, as they say, is history.

What are the takeaways from the Sun story? First, you don't have to be a domain expert to start a business. But you need to know your markets and audience.

Second, people matter. "You may not be the best possible employee," says Shanghvi. "But you have to give your best."

Third, keep quiet until you have something to say. The Sun acquisition of Taro of Israel has been making headlines for some time now because it was a contested takeover. Even now, one of the minority shareholders has not accepted Sun's offer and is holding out for a higher price.

Sun has acquired over 16 companies so far and none of them (has) made the noise that Taro has generated. "I don't make waves," says Shanghvi. "I don't like to take myself too seriously." In the Taro case, he explains, "they went back on their word. That's why we had to become aggressive." Apart from Taro, the foreign companies and interests Sun has acquired include Caraco, Phlox Pharma, various brands from Women's First Health, Able Labs and Chattem – all from the US – and ICN, of Hungary. Taco is based in Israel but has operations in several countries.

Unlike Big Pharma in the West – which will withdraw a life-saving drug or device if it is not making enough money for them – Sun has demonstrated a soul above the bottomline. Since 2003, all shareholders of Sun have been contributing a percentage of their dividends to charity. The first year, Shanghvi's own contribution was ₹5 crore ($909,090).

The Q1 results (April-June 2012) saw Sun register a 64.1 percent improvement in revenues. Net profit was up 68.8 percent. "The company has beaten street estimates," says a report by Karvy Stock Broking. "The Taro merger has been positive."

[BOARowed with permission from *Boar in Boots – A Business Travelogue* by Parthasarathi Swami (Fortytwo Bookz Galaxy, 2012)]

Case Study 2: Forward integration - and stepping sideways

M. Prabhakar Rao, Chairman, NSL Group

Nuziveedu Seeds, established in 1973 by Mandava Venkataramaiah in his home town of Guntur, Andhra Pradesh, stayed a small business till the founder's son M. Prabhakar Rao took it over in 1982 after finishing college at Benares Hindu University. The past 40 years have seen it growing to become India's largest seed company, with a turnover of ₹ 6,000 crore and accounting for one in every four of the 40 million packets of cotton seeds sold in the country. "Once in, it's like a race!" says Prabhakar Rao, who explains why he hasn't got into politics like many of his peers who run business empires in the state. "I don't have the time, I am running a business! I have to watch the competition all the time to understand how to do things better and stay on top."

Prabhakar Rao is an example par excellence of continuously adding new revenue streams to keep building his business. Once he had established a ₹ 650-crore company with supremacy in cotton seeds, he decided to use them to grow his own cotton. NSL Cotton was born, with farms in neighbouring Marathwada district of Maharashtra.

This was a 'unique model', Prabhakar Rao says – with 300,000 hectares under contract farming and a dozen ginning units, a quarter million spindles that can turn out 15 tonnes per day of yarn, 600 looms with a capacity of 100,000 metres per day and a garment facility which can make 20,000 units a day. "Size matters for global survival!" he explains. NSL also helps the farmers in various ways, supplies them with seeds, assures buyback of the crop, and works closely with them to ensure good quality that meets international norms. It also has an integrated cotton farming (ICF) team which gives free technical advice on what pesticide and how much water to use, ensure that they don't use child labour, and implement the cotton buyback agreement. It is part of the UK's Better Cotton Initiative (BCI) too. NSL Cotton pioneered a change in the industry by introducing the first branded cotton in India. It also prides itself on its organic, contamination-controlled and traceable product.

Next came the obvious extension to ginning of the cotton - followed, naturally, by spinning – under another company, NSL Textiles. With the cloth, it got into apparel and now manufactures shirts, too – making it what one manager described as "a C2C group – cotton to clothing!". NSL Textiles has two garment-making units – one its own, in the chairman's home town Guntur, and the other leased, in Hyderabad – and supplies shirts to Zara in Europe. It has also introduced its own brand, Constello London. The capacity to produce 40 million metres of high-value shirting – and some trousering – material, focuses 'very heavily' on international markets. It is setting up its own retail marketing chain of Constello stores, which gives the company greater flexibility and control over the brand, as well as "a heightened ability to keep our finger on the pulse of the market", as its brochure says.

As Satish Kagliwal, managing director of Nath Biogene (India) Ltd in Aurangabad, Maharashtra, says: "Prabhakar Rao has a tremendous success story. Nobody else has been able to go beyond all limits like he has – not even the established players like Mahyco and Rasi! He knows technology and finance, and he has expanded into power, sugar and SEZs, though every diversification is a risk and unrelated diversifications rarely flourish."

But that wasn't all. NSL also went into a number of unrelated diversifications: NSL Power, NSL Sugars, and NSL Infra. "We have been planning and working towards establishing separate legal entities for the different businesses," says Prabhakar Rao.

Moving forward from producing cotton seeds to growing cotton, to textiles and eventually clothing is a fairly straightforward progression. But power? Sugar? Special Economic Zones? "We got into renewable energy for tax planning for the seed business, which was making a good profit," Prabhakar Rao explains. "We had some starting hiccups, but we did a lot of research into the financial returns and kept investing, especially in Tamil Nadu which has a much more favourable policy than Andhra Pradesh. We realised it's a good business – so much so that we didn't even claim the accelerated depreciation benefits!"

But NSL found limitations of availability of equipment in India, and felt the need to bring in better, more efficient technology to get a better RoI (return on investment). NSL Regen Powertech came into being, in collaboration with two Chennai-based entrepreneurs and private equity funding from Indivision of the Future group. Zeroing in on German company Vensys for its technology, it now makes gearless machines that use permanent magnets, and don't need grid power to start, unlike the conventional ones. It also has its own research and development, which has created a prototype it is testing in a pilot project.

From wind to thermal power plants: two separate companies came up. NSL Power is building supercritical plants in Nagapattinam, Tamil Nadu, and Anugul, Orissa, while NSL Renewable Power is concentrating on emerging technologies like wind and solar energy. It also has hydro-electric projects in Himachal Pradesh.

Spreading its wings further, the company has, through an overseas subsidiary, acquired development rights to set up a wind power project in Chile, one of the largest of its kind in Latin America with a potential of over 400 MW when fully developed. On five adjacent sites to be developed in phases, the project involves a total investment of US $650 million over a three-year period. "We are in search of global opportunities in power," says Prabhakar Rao. "This will act as a springboard to capitalise the opportunities in the region." At home, it is looking at nearly 4,000 MW of wind, biomass, hydro-electric and thermal power by 2015. It is also in the process of setting up 2,640 MW of conventional, coal-based plants.

NSL's established expertise in agri-business led to the setting up of NSL Sugars in 2003, with the avowed aim of "playing the role of a game-changer". It has five plants, with a projected total sugar refining capacity of 15,000 tonnes per day (tpd) by 2015. This is a good business to be in: the demand for sugar is always higher than the supply. Focussing on integrated plants that also have power cogeneration and produce ethanol, it targets capacities of 550 MW and 1,700 kilolitres per day over the same time frame. The company is also setting up a refinery to process raw sugar from cane-growing countries like Brazil and exporting it back. NSL Sugars' integrated plants enable it to diversify and maximise its revenue base, giving it the leverage to balance its product lines.

Around the same time, NSL also began buying land. "We made lots of investments between 2004-05 and 2009 from the profits of the seeds business," Prabhakar Rao explains. "We have 1.5 million sq.ft of office space in Hyderabad, mostly occupied by information technology companies," he says. "We plan to build 10 million sq.ft here and in the NCR in the next four to five years." Working in consultation with 'best-in-industry' global experts, it is completing five SEZs in Hyderabad, Chennai and the NCR, besides a number of retail, commercial and residential projects. In different places, it offers 'walk-to-work' homes, gold-rated green buildings, 100-percent power back-up, a car park for every 1,000 sq.ft leasable area and building services for 24x7 hours operations. He predicts a real estate boom now that the vexed, decades-old Telangana issue is settled. NSL Infra already has big multinational corporations like IBM and Wells Fargo occupying its SEZ in Hyderabad. It also plans an IT SEZ in Noida, and is developing a residential project in Chennai and another in Bangalore with local developers.

The group's Mandava Foundation is 'especially proud' of the contribution it is making in the transfer of knowledge to the farmer community. "It is an example of leveraging our core competence and paying back to society with the body of expertise we have acquired over the years," says the group brochure. The Foundation is also working in three other basic need areas — education, health-care and employment generation — in which it can impact society most significantly.

Group founder Venkataramaiah, 80, told his company's magazine *Topseed* that his son had changed the fortunes of the company. His philosophy of "Don't let the farmer down... spend enough time in the fields to understand the ground better" has obviously been adopted by the son. Prabhakar Rao will need to see how his own vision is carried forward, now that his son has also joined the business.

Keep costs under control at all times, not only during recession

There is a famous saying from Warren Buffett: "I stay away from businesses that say, 'we will tighten our belt now' or focus on cost cutting now."

Just like revenue has to be the focus at all times, costs should be the other side of the coin. This is of course easier said than done.

There are classic situations which occur in every entrepreneur's life. This is what I call excess euphoria. Just like the stock market gets momentum once in five years, a business also goes through a cycle of momentum. This is the year the business has an extraordinary growth. Much beyond what was projected and anticipated. The costs are also likely to be low at this point because, remember, the growth was not expected. Now here comes the twist.

Unfortunately, just like in the stock market, extraordinary growth also comes only in extraordinary times or years. Just because you clocked 50 percent growth in one year it is not necessary that you will do so year after year.

Along with growth there is also a cost attached — naturally.

I too, went into this whole cycle unknowingly. We increased our expense drastically in three months anticipating the momentum in the market to continue. Alas! The market crashed and took some big names along with it. The only sensible thing we did was not taking on debt. But we had increased manpower dramatically. When you increase your expenses dramatically you need continuous new business to flow in. You have anticipated big volumes and if that does not materialize, you are in big trouble. This is what happened to India in 2008. I would say a whole lot of companies are still recovering from the contraction in the economy.

Today I am wiser and of course poorer. What are the key lessons I learnt?

There are several revenue heads in business. In our business typically they are:

- Media
- Creative
- Production
- Films
- Events

Some years there may be a big jump in one of the revenue streams. What is worth analysing is, where has this jump come from? From only one client or several clients? If it is only from one client, check why this sudden jump has happened. It could possibly be because of one of many extraordinary events at the customer's place, such as celebrating a centenary, inaugurating a factory, rolling out of the one millionth motorcycle, winning a prestigious award. This revenue is unlikely to occur next year.

When can you consider this as a sustainable revenue stream?

Keep costs under control at all times, not only during recession

When several clients contribute to the revenue;

When your customer has started a new revenue stream which will need sustained activity;

When the customer is expanding and he will need you to upgrade the facility;

When your customer is going international and needs new products or services from you.

A continuous eye on costs is a must.

Many entrepreneurs who are not from business families do not calculate profit and loss on a month-on-month basis. This is a must as it could be too late by the end of the year to know. If you know the month-on-month figures, it is relatively easy to chart out which months are good, which are slow. Also how many permanent employees you need, how many you can take on contract, or on a temporary basis. In most service businesses the biggest cost is employees. Here it is imperative that we continuously monitor productivity. Sometimes Managers inherit legacy systems where the structure is very bloated with too many senior mangers doing the same thing. It is always good to have a policy of hiring freshers who can be on the bench and trained. This is cheaper and helps keep costs under control, not to mention the contribution you are making to your profession and society at large.

The downside to this is that when you have to scale up quickly, this can pose a challenge. However my personal experience says that if you have chosen your freshers wisely they can become productive very quickly. Six months and they can become on par with an employee with three to four years' experience. The key of course is to hire right.

Rents are another area where one can go overboard. Today, with connectivity being so good, no business needs to be in an expensive, tony part of town. Sometimes just being one km away from the hotspot can reduce your real estate cost by over 50 percent. Why not be closer to where your employees reside? Many a time, distance is one of the key factors employees consider before joining a company. Also, with a little smart planning and modular furniture you can have flexible work areas which double up as meeting rooms and conference areas.

The most important place to check costs is to see where productivity is getting lost. One inefficient Manager may be increasing your costs by 10 percent every month. He or she may not begin action on a job on time, may be too soft on getting work done, may not meet deadlines, leading to loss of customers in the long run.

One of the thumb rules we work on is: can you add on clients without dramatically increasing cost?

Exercise:

Work out how many clients you can add without increasing cost

With a little modification in team like taking on an additional 10 freshers, can you increase productivity?

An entrepreneur has to continuously ask the following questions, too:

What should I do? How can I do it? Who can do it? When can it be done? What will be the cost implication? It is a continuous process which is relentless.

You cannot just formulate a system and forget about it. Continuous minor modifications are required as systems in today's scenario become obsolete very quickly.

How to squeeze out maximum revenue with the same cost structure is what needs to be deliberated. Cost controls are critical for the health of any business, but it's not a good idea to arbitrarily cut costs as this may lead to compromise in quality, says Geetanjali Kirloskar, chairperson of Sakra World Hospital in Bangalore. "We must

Geetanjali Kirloskar,
Chairperson, Sakra World Hospital

manage costs, and build cost efficiencies so that the same inputs give more output. The operating theatres, for example, must be able to turn out a larger number of surgeries per day. Also, all your 300 beds being full does not mean that you just have to add beds. Check if the average length of stay per patient can be reduced through more skilled surgeries, better equipment and efficient medical management."

Geetanjali points out that a very high cost component, especially in hospitals, is power. "Can we bring it down from 6 or 7 percent to 4 percent? That's a saving of 33-45 percent under that head. We can, by checking the consumption in high-consumption areas and controlling the wastage there." Medical equipment, in general, consumes a lot of electricity. And when Sakra brought in its new equipment, it all had to undergo trials: "In the beginning, we had everything switched on for hours. Then we realised that if everyone does his or her homework, the necessary testing could be done in one hour at a time," she says. There have been well-meaning suggestions like switching off the power to operating theatres when they are not in use, but that's really counter-productive because the sterile atmosphere needs to be maintained at all times.

Another method is to design your building to maximise power efficiency. Like Sakra's central glass-covered atrium, which increased initial costs by 10 percent but results in 'huge' power savings as it lets in a lot of natural light. The H-shaped design of the building also gives ventilation. The hospital has also installed a hybrid AC so that the air-conditioning can be switched off and on selectively across areas. All this, of course, needed planning in the initial stages, and explained well to the architects and builders. "And in actual use, we all need to be conscious and turn off lights and air-conditioners when we leave a room. It's amazing how a number of people, including patients, leave toilet lights on even in the middle of the day!" Geetanjali adds.

Inventory management is a very important aspect of cost control. In the starting stage of the hospital, business inventory may be 55 days, but should be brought down to 25 days after four months through proper planning, negotiations with vendors and payment schedules. "We get our stents, for instance, on a 'pay by use' model," she explains. "Proper understanding of the movement of medicines is also important."

Manpower costs, too, must be controlled, and productivity increased with proper selection and training. Pilferage can be a big contributor to costs, and strict security measures are essential to tackle this problem. And as in any other business, interest is a big cost – "a vicious spiral", as Geetanjali describes it. "Internal accrual should drive investment," she believes.

Nishit Kumar, who set up the Pune-headquartered NOTRE advertising, public relations and communications group in 1981 at the age of 23, with no business experience or family background, had the going good after his initial troubles. He started with an equity of ₹ 800 - when he ran his office off his mother's dining table, without even a telephone, and took local municipal buses and walked to look for clients. He named it Notre- which means 'our' in French - to reflect the philosophy he still believes in. The agency won many awards, and grew to 10 offices with 337 people. For 14 consecutive years, he became a traveling road show – almost 20 days a month - and brought turnover to ₹ 11 crore. In 1999, however, things started going wrong – horribly so. Some clients' debts went bad. And with the advertising industry working on a wafer-thin margin of 3-4% before tax out of the gross 15 per cent commission on ad costs, expenses went out of hand. "We grew too fast, and I trusted the wrong people!" Nishit says ruefully. "But in hindsight one is always wiser from one's mistakes." To his horror, he discovered that one of his seniormost people, who was heading a big branch, had set up a duplicate company and was raising bills in the name of Notre. Bad debts hit ₹ 7 crore, which had a cascading effect as pressure mounted with banks and media wanting their money. He wound down his operations, retaining only one branch outside Pune: Mumbai, which too is only a representative office. And paid off all those debts, to the last paisa.

"But I decided I would never say die," Nishit says. "I took the hit, learned from experience and started to bounce back." So he got into newer areas: environmental engineering with a new effluent treatment technology, country consultancy to help foreign companies come into India, brand and strategic consulting, and training for corporates. Another major initiative he has started is solutions for schools and colleges, especially in tier-2 and tier-3 cities, to enhance the business and academic performance of schools and colleges country wide.

It is no longer doing advertising releases, but still provides creative and design solutions. "We are a knowledge company which has learnt its lessons," he adds.

Naresh Sareen of Dass Electric points out that when the market demand is suddenly increasing, every businessman plans for taking the maximum share of this growth by expanding his activities and reaching his consumers faster. Unfortunately, however, the zest to grow at times overlooks the long-term disadvantages, and attention is moved from cost to revenue: one forgets that it is best to compete on differentiators rather than price as priority is given to increasing revenues rather than costs.

What happens when the sudden demand that had increased in the market place drops down more suddenly? Are we capable of sustaining such a drop in the top line? Do we have in place a code of conduct to provide guidance on dilemmas that crop up in business? The answer is: No! Because, Naresh explains, one has already established the kind of infrastructure, manpower and expenses to match the growth and the vision. It would be wiser to reduce your fixed expenses and increase your variable expenses. This way, one would be more flexible to swing in tune with the changing market demands.

Narayan Rajan of i-Vista feels that he made 'terrible mistakes' in his spending decisions along the way to building up his business. Scaling up and trying to build capacity on the anvil of new business that was coming in, he didn't have time to see if his growth was hockey-stick shaped, flat or even negative. And just when you think you are off the curve and it won't hit you any longer, it very often comes back and does!

Later, however, he got into another business, Nautilus Shipping, in 2007. Here, his partner concentrates on business acquisition, while Narayan himself plays the role of the finance person. He has created financial discipline, with a structure and a proper plan, and doesn't let any 'splurging' happen. And finally, he has realised that money in the bank is good. When running your own business, he says, you need to focus on the business and the customers; but you always need a strong partner or senior employee with the ability to challenge your every buying decision, and question every expense you make.

Other pitfalls

Before hiring an expensive resource, check the person's track record. Why is he asking for a 50 percent jump? Was he undervalued in his last job or was he worth only that much? Unfortunately there is no foolproof method to gauge this other than discovering how good the candidate is only after hiring him. No amount of reference checks and tests can accurately evaluate what an employee is really worth. The only parameter we have is the track record he brings with him and the potential he has which has not been discovered.

Keep costs under control at all times, not only during recession

Be clear as to why are you hiring him - not only to yourself but also to the candidate concerned:

- For systems and process
- For scaling up
- To take the business to the next level
- To handle a new revenue stream
- To head a department.

Unless you check productivity vs cost, the chances are that your expenses will get bloated very quickly and revenue will not match expenses.

Exercise:

- Check expenses department-wise year on year with corresponding revenue.
- The only reason expense can be more than revenue is if you are clear that you are investing for scale and it will take time to make money.
- Check people vs productivity as per the parameters laid down by your industry.
- Quantify all deliverables by key team including time sheet, training calendars, month on month revenue vs expense.
- Check manpower requirement, overheads in terms of increments and the value they are bringing to the table with the enhanced salary.
- Check what can be outsourced, especially if it is a one-time thing or something you need occasionally.

Exercise:

Month on month, check expenses. If there is an extraordinary expense understand why it happened.

If there is a seasonal dip in your business, can you introduce a new revenue stream which balances out work and revenue without too much incremental cost?

- A mall has flea markets for additional revenue.

- A school can have a fete which can bring additional revenue.

- A publication can have a special wedding supplement or Diwali issue.

When brand specialist Harish Bijoor once asked an audience of mediapersons to say the first thing that came to mind when he said 'Kingfisher', one young man finally said, after a lot of thinking and prodding: "Beer." Harish turned to the women: "Trust a guy to say that! Come on, ladies – what does it make you think of?" One said: "Airline." And that, as Harish points out, is the beauty of branding: nobody seems to remember any longer that the kingfisher is a bird, and a beautiful one at that. But branding apart, Dr Vijay Mallya's Kingfisher Airlines came crashing to the ground – the biggest failure in Indian business, with unpaid loans totalling ₹ 7,000 crore. Was it only because of a failure to keep a tab on expenses, offering every passenger giveaways like a ballpoint pen and headphones in a zippered pouch, and individual television screens? But that's another book!

Interview: G. V. Krishna Reddy, Chairman, GVK Group

Successive US Presidents, all the way back to George Washington, have understood the importance of roads. In fact Washington said in 1785, even before he became the first President, that the great roads leading from one public place to another should be straightened and established by law. What is it like in India?

Infrastructure is the only thing to build and develop any country. Unfortunately, it is not getting as much attention as it should in India. The lack of proper planning is taking the economics of the business from bad to worse. Without planning, the market is just not there any longer! We were the pioneers in laying the first six-lane road project under the public private partnership (PPP) model. We built the 90-km Jaipur-Kishangarh Expressway, an access-controlled toll road connecting Rajasthan's capital to the state's marble capital, as part of the Golden Quadrilateral project. We finished it six months ahead of schedule, and it was inaugurated in April 2005. It was a BOT (build-operate-transfer) project, which we completed at a cost of ₹ 729 crore.

But the conditions imposed on road developers are unbearable. I have to own a certain percentage of equity till the specified period is over. I have put in equity for one, two, three projects – but I can't go on doing this. I'm not allowed to sell. A real estate man builds a project, sells it and moves on – this should happen with roads, too.

How long can we hold them beyond a limit? But now we are all hopeful because there is a dynamic new man as Chairman of the National Highways Authority of India (NHAI). He has taken up strongly for a rule change to allow selling projects.

Otherwise, infrastructure is in great trouble because all the money we developers have put in has dried up.

What about electricity? There is a lot of trouble regarding the availability of natural gas, without which the independent power producers are finding their costs going up.

The country needs lots of power for growth. But the shocks have been the worst in power plants. This is the first sector that came up after liberalisation began in 1991. India invited people from all over the world to come and invest here. We were again the pioneers: we set up the first power plant, at Jegurupadu near Rajahmundry. But it ran into opposition right at the beginning. The land was allotted later, and we commissioned the first phase of the 217-MW CCPP (combined cycle power plant) in 1997, creating a benchmark for private power plants. Our design improves operational efficiencies and reduces environmental impact. We have planted so many trees and plants around it that it has been described as a "horticulture project that also generates electricity".

This was the only project financed by the IFC (International Finance Corporation) in Washington, which was the lead financial institution. The World Bank, IFC's parent, even honoured me for completing the project. But the government backed down from its commitment to supply natural gas to operate the plant. It also refused to pay GVK to use naphtha as an alternative fuel, even though that was legally agreed. I had to operate without profit, paying all my fixed charges of loan interest, establishment charges and so on. Even worse, with zero gas supply, they are now imposing legal penalties on us for not providing power! How can I fight the government if it breaks the law itself?

Only the Gujarat government imports LNG (liquefied natural gas). They saw the future, and built a terminal. But Andhra Pradesh has not done anything, even though GVK is prepared to set it up. The government must pay fixed charges to save the sector from ruin, till the Krishna-Godavari basin gas becomes available after two years. I really don't want to touch the power sector anymore.

But you are very proud of your airports, especially the new second terminal in Mumbai. How did you go about implementing that project?

Isn't it unbelievable that we could create a totally new terminal in the city? The government had asked us only to expand and refurbish the existing one. They laughed at our suggestion to totally build a new terminal. Now, we have created something that will last for at least the next 60 years – beyond my lifetime, even my son's, but for the people of Mumbai! We moved not only the Air-India and Indian Airlines facilities that were in the way. We also shifted a number of small temples, a police station - and even a statue of Chhatrapati Shivaji, after whom the airport is named. We took everyone to the site, and persuaded politicians from all parties that this was necessary to build one of the best airports in the world. And that is what we have finally built.

More than 50,000 tonnes of steel have gone into the terminal. But none of it is visible anywhere throughout the building. The car park can accommodate 5,200 vehicles. It is the biggest in India. The new elevated road over the slums nearby has cut driving time to three minutes. Earlier, it would take half an hour to 40 minutes! And the drive between the domestic and international airports is only 15 minutes. Even this will not be necessary after we shift the present domestic terminal to the new one. The old building will be demolished to create more runways. We also have the first right of refusal for the proposed Navi Mumbai airport. And abroad, we are developing two more international airports in Indonesia.

How is the hotel business doing, especially in today's situation of too many rooms chasing too few customers?

We run our hotels in collaboration with the Taj Group. We have a joint venture, Taj GVK Hotels & Resorts Ltd. My wife Indira Reddy is Managing Director. The company is 14 years old, and has six properties in Hyderabad. Two more are being developed, at Mumbai airport and in Bangalore. These are doing well, even though the economy is not great — especially in Hyderabad. We are paying off loans and reducing the interest burden. So the balance sheet will improve.

You also have a health sciences company. How healthy are its finances?

GVK Biosciences is also doing well. It has cutting-edge infrastructure that supports the high quality of its research. It has about 250,000 sq.ft of laboratory space and facilities in Hyderabad, Gurgaon and Ahmedabad. Its research centres are supported by attached state-of-the-art analytical, support and ancillary functions. It also has offices in the US and Singapore.

We are not the only ones, every infrastructure company has burnt its fingers.

We need to move very fast, change things drastically to carry the country along. India has a big future. There is a lot more to do. But we have fallen behind by 20-30 years.

Case Study: Advantages become disadvantages

E. Sudhir Reddy, CMD, IVRCL

IVRCL is another infrastructure group that is trying to buck the downward trend in the infrastructure industry by getting out of a number of unviable road projects and concentrating on manufacturing and design.

E. Sudhir Reddy, Chairman and Managing Director, IVRCL, says manufacturing is the future. Having burnt his fingers in infrastructure like GVK and so many others in the sector, he explains how group companies HDO and Davy Markham have taken the Group into very high-end, critical products, helping to pull it out of the red. Infrastructure is a 'big basket', confusing roads with power and coal, and the construction industry is on the verge of becoming sick, too. Every company that had planned growth in the field has become the owner of assets which they are all trying to sell.

Over the years, IVRCL invested in design teams and human capital - but the ultra-mega road projects haven't seen the light of day, so the investment has been 'wasted', Reddy says: "My advantage has become a disadvantage!" For the past couple of years, the order book was two to two-and-a-half times its trailing revenue. About one-third of it was expected to be converted into turnover. "But it's not happening," Sudhir Reddy says. "We've now upped it to three-and-a-half times to four times the trailing revenue, so that we can convert 18 per cent – but there is an execution risk, as we need to maintain 8,000 people when we sit on orders worth ₹ 26,000-28,000 crore."

There is a 'clog' in the system, he complains: it needs a kickstart to get going again.

IVRCL has merged all its road assets, worth ₹ 700-plus crore in the process of redesigning all its assets - both human capital and physical. This will bring in cash, which it needs. Facing the same problem as GVK, it has sold large parts of three road projects, and has now sought NHAI's permission to allow it to sell 100 per cent of two completed roads. "We must have an ombudsman at the very top for BOT (build, operate, transfer) projects, like AAI (Airports Authority of India) which allowed a 329-per-cent hike in Delhi airport's charges," Sudhir Reddy says.

Financial analysts say recovery is still far off, because of policy inaction. The company's fund flow is poor. This can block up to 20 per cent because the last bit of money doesn't come. And without very deep pockets, it needs external funding: support from financial institutions and the banking sector. IVRCL has sacked 500 employees, and is cutting other costs on things like guest houses and cars. But recognising that it is still a people business, it is the first infrastructure company to have offered employee stock options (ESOPs), distributing over three million shares "to appreciate our employees' contribution and ensure they share in our success".

The company grew at around 50 per cent CAGR over the past 10 years, but order conversion slowed down over the past couple of years. This is mainly because of delays in government decisions like payment release approvals. This increases receivables, and creates a vicious circle: IVRCL has an order book worth ₹28,000 crore, but conversion has dropped from 40 per cent to just 25 per cent in 2012. All industries dealing with the government are facing a slowdown, but infrastructure is affected more than the rest. With the stated corporate aim "We Make It Happen", the big question for Sudhir Reddy is, when it will happen.

Enrolment of key people for the next level

Why is it that some businesses cannot scale up? The answer could be that key people who have been with you for several years may be the impediment to you reaching the next ₹ 100 crore.

Once the vision is set we need to make it happen…

Breaking down the vision into smaller steps always helps. A good example of this is, what is your vision statement?

Ours is

To be a world-class company offering cutting edge strategy and creative solutions to build profitable brands.

So then what is our Mission?

To think, create and build brands.

What is our goal?

To build five brands in a year

All this means that we need to live this vision, mission and goal every single day.

It is definitely not okay just to stick it up on the walls, although it most definitely helps. What is most important is to live and breathe it.

This translates into hiring or retraining people to be aligned with the vision. Attracting clients who will contribute to the above and producing works which will live up to the standards we have set for ourselves.

But in most companies there is a big disconnect, that the vision has not percolated down. From our own experience we have seen that setting the vision is like setting a strategy; but setting the strategy without a game plan is tantamount to it never being executed. So once the strategy is set – let's say, to reach ₹ 100 crore in 3 years - what is essential is to set the game plan.

So how should the game plan read? What is a game plan? It is nothing but how you can reach your target.

If your vision is to be a world-class company you have to understand what constitutes world class.

Let me list some qualities. You can add your own.

1. Best practices from around the globe

2. Global quality standard measured against an industry benchmark

3. People drawn from the best universities

4. Response time of say 24 hours

5. Winning x number of awards

6. Being amongst the top 20 in your industry—depending on which industry. Your goal may be to be in the top three.

Define profitable brands

So as a company you are not only building brands; but what kind of brands are you defining? One of the key benchmarks against which you will measure your success is whether the product or service has become a brand, and if it is successful. Is it profitable? What is the turnover of the brand? Have you checked the balance sheet of the company? I am defining just one step to drive home the point that it is not only about setting strategy but also having a game plan and somebody driving it actively. Finally, whatever you decide you want to do, there should be ownership from you or somebody assigned in the team to drive it. I remember Steve Ballmer who was then COO of Microsoft, saying that a leader has to drive, drive, drive. It was a very powerful visual, backed with how passionately he said it. Aggressive drivers like Steve Ballmer have a particular style which may not necessarily be followed by everybody. There are different management styles. I will immediately put in a disclaimer that it is one style of management and each company will have its own.

Along the way I discovered one very important thing. Organizations have to be frequently broken and recreated to achieve scale and bring in world class. After all what is ageing? In my dictionary it is nothing but doing the same thing over and over again. As the organization is changing direction it is important that people also undergo transformation to align themselves with its pace. Otherwise, there is a danger of having a poor driver behind the wheel of a 2000cc 150bhp-engined car. That would be very tragic.

Having said all this, how do you ensure that the strategy, the vision, percolates down the organization? One of the key things is enrolment of key drivers into this process. So how do you enrol them? Why can't you have one forceful method of just implementing it? I believe it's because each person is different and one method does not fit all. Yes, there will be general rules and regulations which can be templatized; but the vision is something creative. This should ideally be explained one to one among the key team so that they have a chance to voice their concerns which you can address. This way we have a chance to access the wisdom of the team. But the main point here is not all this. It is — are the main drivers aligned to the vision? Have they embraced it as their own? Are they passionately involved in it?

Most of the times it so happens that we are unable to persuade people who have been with us for a decade or so to buy into the new vision. They are happy with the status quo and do not wish to upset the apple cart. Why break a perfectly functioning system and recreate? But I have seen that it is better to break the status quo and create something new — whether it is an outdated process, system of doing things or a division. I would rather do it voluntarily than be forced to do it. Unfortunately, in life there is nothing like maintenance mode ... what we call maintenance mode is slow decline.

Dayanand Agarwal,
Founder Chairman, DRS Group,
Hyderabad

Some entrepreneurs and their companies are lucky. The DRS Group in Hyderabad, which runs India's biggest household goods moving firm Agarwal Packers & Movers, has a team of employees – from the Chairman's personal assistant to packers, loaders and drivers – who have been with it since its inception in 1988 and have taken it forward along founder Dayanand Agarwal's mapped lines of growth.

The same applies to the MH Group in Jabalpur, a fourth-generation business with 50 factories around the country producing five crore hand-rolled bidis every day. MH's oldest employee is 82-year-old Himmatbhai Shah, who joined as a driver of the family patriarch's

Siddharth Patel
Managing Director, MH Group,
Jabalpur

Bentley car – and is now the chief accountant, with 62 years of service behind him. His son Shirish Shah has also joined MH, and looks after the Group's tea division. Says current Managing Director Siddharth Patel, who is all set to hand over the business to his sons Kanishka and Aditya: "Many others have been with us for three generations. All of them have bought into our vision of taking the business forward, including the diversification into consumer goods like tea."

Definition of maintenance mode - being on auto pilot or status quo. No new learning. Shining and living on the grace of your manager.

So now the question is: how do you enrol key people?

How do you align the entire key team to the new vision?

How do you whip out a sterling performance from people who have been there and done that?

How do you whip up excitement?

How do you ensure that the next rung of people and finally the entire company buy and live the vision?

Here I would like to acknowledge a very powerful exercise we learnt from Verne Harnish, author of a workshop on Strategy and Execution, called 'Start..........stop.........continue'

The principal benefit of this exercise is that it aligns people with the organisational goals. The solutions come from the team. It breaks down strategy into practical execution which people can relate to and have a time line for. This needs to be done every week for best results. The team learns to take charge.

This works very well in organizations where the entrepreneur ends up doing everything leaving him with no time for core business.

It brings people on the same page where they actively participate in driving the game plan.

It is a fairly simple exercise but needs to be done diligently. This is one way the strategy can be viewed every week by the entire key team and simplified enough for people to follow and align with what needs to be done.

So if one of the strategies is to reach ₹ 100 crore we get the collective wisdom of the group. About 10 people in a group is ideal but I guess it can go up to 20.

What should we as a company start doing? Some responses typically will be:

- Start improving the sales funnel
- Start getting aggressive
- Start improving response time
- Start with a website
- Start attending industry seminars.

What should we stop doing?

- Stop procrastinating
- Stop resisting

It is unbelievable how 'Stop Resisting' comes up in every collective wisdom meeting. In our company we call this group the Council.

Example:

Challenge - How to create something new

Start	Stop	Continue	Action points
How to make a brief look cool by bringing energy	Resisting	Being enthusiastic	Add humor and trust your team member
Start connecting unrelated things	Being mentally lazy		Follow 'A' creative method of thinking
Provocation disruption to perform better	Templatized thinking		Brainstorming sessions at outbound locations at 6.30 am
Working together as a team			Incorporate buddy system

Note: in our company we added 'Action point' as week after week we were doing start stop and continue without any visible implementation.

"As a CEO, I spent a considerable amount of time in recruiting divisional heads reporting to me after off loading the wrong people and it paid me in achieving my planned growth," says Venkat Changavalli, Leadership Mentor, Management Consultant, Trainer and Inspirational Speaker who set up and ran the pioneering '108' ambulance service EMRI. "I percolated the corporate vision of saving a million lives every year at the ambulance level by translating that every ambulance makes on an average 2,000 trips per annum (at the rate of six per day)— and if 5 percent of these trips are for very critical patients, each ambulance would save 100 lives every year. Nationally, if 10,000 ambulances operate, the vision of saving one million lives every year becomes a reality at this rate."

Dr. Santanu Paul,
CEO and MD, TalentSprint

Adds TalentSprint CEO and MD Dr. Santanu Paul: "As a leader, I look at enrolment of key people as a fundamental step in implementing any strategy or even a significant change in direction. The days of top-down, command and control management are definitely over. If we want smart, creative team members to work with us to build an enterprise, we cannot expect them to be blind order-takers. So instead of ordering them, we have to 'recruit' or 'enrol' them into the cause. They have to see and appreciate the big picture just as much as the leader, and they have to feel a strong desire to personally connect with and contribute to it.

"A metaphor that has always helped me is to think of my role as that of an orchestra conductor with a hundred different instrument players at my disposal. This is in complete contrast to a more traditional metaphor of a military commander who wants every soldier to move in the same way in the same direction. As an orchestra conductor, I have to accommodate the differing instruments, competencies, styles, and preferences of each player. Only when I fully comprehend and empathize with what each player brings to the stage can I coax them all to play the masterpiece together, each in their own way adding to the beauty and perfection of the overall outcome. To ask everyone to play the same instrument in the same way cannot produce a grand audience experience, it can at best produce bland compliance and a mediocre performance."

As Business Coach Ujjal Gupta says, the key element of business growth is people, the right kind of people. Having this key resource is of greater importance than other elements like market opportunities. When the business needs to step up to the next level, the top leadership will provide the vision. This vision will be converted into strategy by the senior management and, most importantly, the strategy must get implemented on the ground. "This is where most plans for business growth die quick deaths. For effective implementation of strategy, the business needs effective people at the appropriate levels," Ujjal points out.

More often than not, the existing staff cannot step themselves up in line with the growth objectives of the business. When the business is seeking movement to the next level, and not just a normal rate of growth, people at the implementation level (middle management and lower) need to buy into the vision and have the capability of going to that next level themselves. Existing people often would prefer status quo, will not do anything different and will try to remain in their comfort zones. It therefore becomes an essential element of growth strategy to get the right people into the system and let go of those existing staff members who will not measure up to the needs of the future.

The difficulty comes in the transition phase. The business will need to hire the right persons and they will come at market rates which will be way above the current compensation levels of existing staff. Top leadership will face the challenge of differential pay scales within the system and the risk of escalating staff costs at all levels.

Lastly, what should we continue doing?

If you as a company have been around for a couple of years surely you have been doing some things right. So you need to continue doing what is working.

With this one exercise in our company we have managed to whip up unprecedented excitement. For the first time we realized that people are actually giving suggestions and participating in meetings.

After practising this for a month we realized that all it needs is a gameplan.

For example a suggestion could be to start getting aggressive in sales... so we need to put a game plan immediately next to that agenda.

Start getting aggressive in sales – make a game plan; put a website together if you don't have one, get it SEO compliant if you have one. Put a budget for SEM. Make flyers. Attend seminars – list which ones. Allocate a budget, a time frame and the driver.

Example 1

Start improving response time

Game plan:

Revert within three hours

If it is not possible to deliver, tell customer in advance

Proactively ask customers what is the likely schedule which will come up every Monday, Wednesday, Friday. This cuts a lot of emergency jobs which come up in an organization, especially if you are in the service industry.

Example 2

Improve quality

Game plan:

Understand the job in totality. Are you clear about what needs to be delivered? Who will handle the job? What are the checks and balances you will keep in mind? Who will do the quality check at the end? What is the time frame? A driver needs to be added in every game plan.

So in enrolment, the prerequisites are as follows:

Clarity in what you intend to do

Where you want to take the company

Why you want to do what you want to do

What is the result you wish will happen

How you intend it will happen

What will happen if you do not do it.

How do you see the person you wish to enrol executing any part of the strategy?

What is in it for her? How will it benefit her? Can you help him visualize his future with this new plan? If he is able to visualize the benefits is the job done? What if he is unable to? Then you have to start a full-fledged war and find ways and means to open out the possibilities. It could be articles, workshops, industry seminars, etc which will help a person start accepting the new reality. One can work from threat or benefit perception. Definitely choosing the latter is wiser in the long run.

"Business is about building relations, Organization is about relating with what is to be built.

Visions build business and relations build an Organization.

Competition is due to lack of a vision.

Vision is not just a statement, or even a state, it is the spirit of the whole business.

Business which is progressive lasts long and not the one which is merely profitable.

Profitable business creates competitions, progressive business brings innovation — Sanjay Thakker, creator of Corporate SSY

Now what if you cannot enrol key members? Of course my take on that is very simple — if you have not enrolled key members it is because of your own lack of enthusiasm. Somewhere you are not enrolled in your own strategy and vision for what you want to achieve.

But now for argument's sake, since this is a book replete with case studies, what if you did not enrol the right people?

Your key team members will become the biggest impediment to reach the size and scale you want to. Every move you make in the direction will be thwarted. Why is that so?

Contrary to what people say organizations are run mainly on co-operation and not competition. Sure, there will be pockets of competition which may not be healthy; but finally an organization runs on a team that works together. It is more like a relay race rather than a 100-metre dash where one individual is glorified. So in very simple terms the baton will not be passed on quick enough to the next person - and there goes the grandest of visions, trampled to the ground. One more bites the dust.

So from time to time companies should do a people audit to see if the current set of people we have can be taken to the next level. Are they enthusiastic?

Do they still have hunger to learn something new?

Are they excited about adventure and venturing into unknown fields?

After all, nothing fails like success. A couple of good years make a company soft and lose that appetite to win new business where you may have to do all it takes to be a winner.

Beware also of some kind of people, especially people in sales, who work in a company like a fixed deposit (FD)... they work well for the first couple of years — those years when they were hungry, lucky, the economy was good, there were takers for the company's products and services. They have won their bonus and brownie points. Soon, they relax. I believe that they genuinely think it is an FD, forgetting that it needs to be replenished every day or else you will only be drawing out of that Fixed Deposit and not replenishing it enough. So as an entrepreneur you need to ensure that your people are also growing to the next level along with you. Train in numbers. After all, an organization is finally nothing but a collection of people with different energy levels.

Show people the vision and the future and keep your own energy and enthusiasm levels high so you can enrol and align people to the organization goals.

Interview: Suhas Baxi, Former CEO, Pennar Industries Ltd

How important would you say it is to have the right person in the right job?

It's vital. You can't get anywhere without ensuring that. When I took over in this position in Hyderabad, for instance, I was immediately faced with an uphill task - that of changing the mindset of the older employees so that the company can achieve its ambitious goal to transform itself in the next five years from a me-too steel producer into an eminent engineering company. We had many people whose experience told them that the old ways had worked fine. Pennar has traditionally been a steel producer, so rejections have always been looked at in terms of percentage. Today, we have far more demanding customers. There is one that makes automotive components, which measures quality in ppm (parts per million). But for our older employees, this is not a significant customer, as it needs only 1200 tonnes of steel for 1 million parts. So where the oldies were thinking 'only so much steel', the customer was looking at a million parts. So what happened was that we were losing business. Eventually, we managed to convince our people that the paradigms have changed. We now have a former TVS person heading our industrial components business, and we can ensure perfect on-time, in-full delivery.

Did you manage to convince everyone, or did you have to take more drastic measures?

The transition was painful and arduous. Obviously, we had to make difficult decisions. Many people had been in the company for years, and the founder Chairman Mr Nrupender Rao could not ask them to leave. There was no retirement policy, which means that we had an average employee age of 50-60 years. I had to talk to many people my father's age, who were among the earliest employees and had been around since the company was set up 25 years ago. Yes, there was a huge level of trust and camaraderie among them — but that's not enough to take the company forward the way we want to go. So we needed to identify the people with the right abilities whom we need over the next 15 to 30 years. The new leadership team, with 12 people from different parts of the country, is capable of doing this.

And where are you taking Pennar with this new team?

The current turnover across our six business segments is ₹ 1,500 crore. Our target is double the top line to ₹ 3,000 crore in the current financial year, 2013-14. By 2018, we must take the Group to the US$1-billion mark.

Case Study: Recruiting right

Ujjal Gupta, Business Coach

During my days in HMV, I had seen the impact of recruiting the right people at senior levels with out-of-scale compensation packages. The company went from a ₹ 20-crore business to a ₹ 100-crore entity in a matter of four years in the early 1990s. On the other hand, in my consulting days, I have seen business owners having ambitious plans to grow five — fold in five years, but they could not make the transition to enrol the right people at the right salaries for fear of upsetting the apple-cart of existing human resources.

Exercise:

1. Check new business regularly...no slacking, check value of new clients coming. Value going out. Why are they going out if they are? Who to check with? Business Development Head.

2. People...rotation, right man for the right job, are people growing or stagnating? Are they adding value? Check with Human Resource and double check with operations?

3. Question each team leader every fortnight. Ensure you are not being managed. The only thing to do is ask questions. See questions below.

4. Keep a close eye on the people who manage the business on an everyday business. See if they are at the peak of their professions or have stopped learning.

How would you know they have stopped learning? When they start blaming everybody other than themselves for the challenges happening around them. Could be minor ones also.

Questions to ask the team members:

These are useful in ensuring that you are not being managed by your team members. You must have a series of 10 questions ready at all times.

Common statement made by your key team members to manage you.

I am following up the payment. It is under process.

They are signing the contract. (Please note there is no definite date).

I have told him (subordinate) several times. He is still not getting it.

Yes I am doing that. (You have no mail, no confirmation it is happening).

Client is happy. Everything is under control.

Things are happening.

When people don't mention specifics, like date, time, name of person, amount, specific names, exactly where the job is stuck, it's very safe to assume you are being managed.

So what are the questions which need to be asked?

1. Client is happy.

    Your questions

    I am planning to speak to the client. Is there anything I need to know?

2. Yes we have booked the revenue.

   You: But I do not think we have delivered any job to him

   Your questions

   Specifically can you tell me 1, 2, 3 jobs delivered/worked on and which of the team members have done what?

3. The bills have gone...

   Your questions

   When did they go? For what amount. Who did you deliver them to? Do you have a stamp? When is the payment expected? How much is expected?

   3a. Have all supporting documents for the bill gone?

   What are the supporting documents? A random check may be required.

4. We are following all processes.

   Your questions

   Are you following the planning sheet? How often, and is everybody following it?

5. The briefing is happening properly.

   Your questions

   How often is it happening? Is it in depth enough? Are you adding the research component to the brief, what about referral images, have you added client hygiene?

6. The job will be delivered today.

   Your questions

   Will the total job be delivered, or in parts? Who is working on it? What is the exact time it will be delivered? How will it be delivered? By whom? In what format?

You get the drift. Does this mean you are micro managing? I don't think so. Many times I sincerely think that entrepreneurs need to be on top of everything. Even the most trusted managers start managing you. Why do they start managing you? It is convenient for you to not ask too many questions as you are busy with a whole bunch of other happenings.

Why does a manager manage things?

In my opinion it is because of his badge of position. Once you reach a position of seniority you cannot show you do not know. So what is the next best thing you do? You pretend you know. So what is the natural expression of pretending you know? You manage or pretend to yourself you are managing and are on top of things. She or he may be allowing themselves also to be managed by their subordinates. So your Manager may be as much a victim of circumstances as you are. But in a fast moving business who is interested in victims? Certainly not the client, or you. What does the client want? Solutions and Delivery which you need to provide in the most efficient and cost effective way you can possibly manage.

Your questions

How much is total exposure? How much is over 60 days? How much is coming? When do you expect rest to come? What are you doing to collect next tranche? Will you continue work if payment has not come in?

Client is under control

Which job is being handled, what was the last delivery, was he unhappy about something? Is he happy about anything. What are his specific complaints? (trick question). What has been his specific praise for if at all.

We have sent many proposals

Who have you sent to? What was the amount in the proposal? Why should they give us the job?

You get the drift.

How often should you do this?

Twice a week at bare minimum. Unfortunately. Your eye can never ever be off the ball. 15 days also can prove fatal which can give you a setback of 3 months.

Now you may be wanting to ask - will I be stuck with this for the rest of my life?

You need to do this till the day you have a super efficient operations person who is like your counterpart. Even then I am of the opinion you need to be in the questioning mode.

Continuous learning

Today's business environment is about continuous learning. Let's just put it this way – it is one never-ending saga which goes on and on. Business is relentless. Every so often a company reaches or exceeds its sales target and guess what happens. The next year there may be a slide. Why do you think it happens? Sanjay Thakker, Founder of Corporate SSY, says "For most people on achievement of target, it is over... the neural pattern in the brain is hardwired to the phenomenon that there is a start and end event. So on achievement of a target the brain neural pattern recognizes it as being over."

So how do you ensure an environment of continuous learning in an organization?

Also why is continuous learning required? These are all perplexing questions but need an answer. Unfortunately, the freshers who pass out of college today have worked very hard to finish their last semester and just want that goal to be over and done with before they start a fresh chapter; and tragically, very few institutes have taught students one basic thing: that passing out of a college or institute is only one part of the story. The real journey begins now. Nobody teaches them that they need to keep learning to go to the next level. Most people think that having passed in flying colours there is really nothing more to learn. What a misconception that is!

I would say that any manager/entrepreneur has to be ready, willing and enthusiastic about learning something every day. The biggest failures happen after a hugely successful year.

Success is a poor teacher. It only makes you arrogant and you get into a zone where you are not listening to anybody. .

We realized that we had got into that rut in our own company too. When you have been around for a decade, handled several verticals, worked with some of the best Indian and multinational companies, you definitely think that you have done a lot and seen a lot. But guess what? After some failures we realized that every project has to be taken up as if we had never done it before. The past can only be a reference point, you cannot base an entire new presentation or strategy on what you have done before even if it is for the same category. We realized that we need to approach it with childlike enthusiasm and a "tell me more" attitude. This gives dramatic results.

Then the thinking is fresh and also you give this very powerful message down the organization that you had better be learning everyday; or you become history. It forces you to renew yourself periodically and keep reinventing yourself.

I would also like to discuss templatization here: when we say templatization what I mean to say is standardizing and putting things in a format which then is scalable and can be replicated by the juniors. While this is a must for scale, no question about it, what happens somewhere down the line is very dangerous. The people who put in the template get so carried away that their thinking becomes templatized. This is the beginning of the end.

Templates are meant to help juniors or non-thinkers to achieve standardization, it is not for the original thinker to stop innovating. The very purpose of templatization is so the chief creative person can create and move to other things.

Chief creative thinker - who is this? This could refer to a person or group of people in an organization who create new revenue streams, strategies, innovations, new ideas, new thinking. They may also be termed as 'intraprenuers'. Intraprenuers focus on innovation and creativity, and transform an idea into a profitable venture while operating within the organisational environment.

Unfortunately templatization works in such a way that people who create also get carried away by this. Organizations should have strict processes for this, and check every six months whether the watertight template is still working or needs to be reworked as per current market conditions or new revenue streams which have come into the system.

Check if the original thinkers are innovating enough. After all why did templatization come in?

To build scale.

To free thinkers from regular day-to-day activity which can easily be done by the operations or execution team.

To ensure that newer innovations happen in the company. After all, as seen in the earlier chapter new revenue streams are a given in today's world.

How do you learn continuously? Isn't it enough that you are VP, CEO or whatever?

What is the meaning of Narayanamurthy's statement 'At every level of Infosys I had to first scale to the next level'? The head of the organization first has to mentally expand his consciousness to go to the next level. A famous quote: "When the student is ready the master appears."

When we admit that we do not have the skill set for the next level, we automatically start our search for the right seminars, speakers, books which will help us scale up. Nobody has ever 'arrived' in business. One of the biggest fallacies is thinking, 'this is it.' Unfortunately, it is never 'it'.

All this is easier said than done. The head of the organization may still be in a continuous learning mode but what about the rest of the managers? Can you say the same about your team? Or departmental heads of other divisions? For an organization to move ahead teams have to make music together. Here I believe that one important thing can ensure continuous learning. And that one thing is: TRUST.

Every team member should feel trusted and that trust should come from the leader who allows people to fail. Let me clarify here. What is failure? It is a result. Why does one fail? One of the reasons is that you do not know enough about something or you have no mastery of it. That is the simplest definition, right? What if the team leader provides a trusting and nurturing environment where the team members can admit their ignorance? They can admit that they do not know? That they are willing and eager to learn?

We have realized all these truths in our own organization. Why do team leaders get into hiding their inefficiencies? They do not feel trusted by the organization to show their vulnerability. Soon the energy of the entire organization will be the same. Where nobody knows, they are not willing to admit this nor are they willing to learn. How can they learn when they have not admitted this even to themselves? Now imagine a company like this. Is it a recipe for disaster or what?

Why do some of the best companies become history?

Why do they not listen to what Mr Market is telling them?

Why are they too arrogant to listen to feedback?

Why are they not investing in learning?

Do take time to answer these questions. That company which is not growing could very well be yours.

Make a list of the companies which have been consigned to history. Why has it happened?

Every tenet of business - whether it is financial literacy, knowing market trends, customers or focus - can be learnt. There are any number of seminars on various subjects from Success principles to Execution methodology.

I can recommend some good ones:

Strategy and Execution - Verne Harnish

Lateral Thinking - Edward De Bono

Chanakya - Radhakrishna

Ten Success Principles - Jack Canfield

Leader without a Title - Robin Sharma

Also read Ram Charan, Larry Bossidy.

Seminars keep happening in most Indian cities. They are a very good investment. You will always have two or three takeaways which you can incorporate in your organization. Invest in good management books. An author is a thought leader and it is interesting to read a person's take on any subject be it strategy, differentiators, execution, team handling, or innovation.

The ability to learn is to the business world what adaptability is to the biological world, says Dr. Santanu Paul, CEO and MD, Talent Sprint. It is the strongest indicator of fitness, which enables a firm to successfully survive, propagate and grow. The biggest and strongest may not survive over time, but those who learn faster than others definitely will. Too often, business leaders spend a huge amount of time belabouring and berating their team members on HOW they should do things. This is a colossal waste of leadership energy. In my experience, most people, given the context and the right amount of information, can figure out HOW to do things on their own. So in essence, a leader should not obsess too much about HOW questions.

Instead, leaders who want their team members to grow and stretch and step up must spend time with them asking WHY and WHAT questions. WHY is the mother of all questions. The more we force our team members to ask these questions, the more they become curious, and the more they learn on their own.

For example, instead of simply giving someone a preset sales target, first ask the person WHAT they think the firm's sales target range ought to be this year, WHY they think such a target range is important, and WHAT they think their own target therefore ought to be. Then sit back and watch their thinking evolve. You will see their brain machinery clicking into motion, you will hear the gears turning, and then you will see them start to ask far deeper questions about company goals and targets than they ever did when you handed them those preset targets. "Once you set such a culture of curiosity in motion, you are no longer the only one figuring out why, what, how, who, when and where; there are a hundred others sharing accountability with you," Dr Paul adds.

Says Ujjal Gupta, Business Coach: "The saying goes, 'Change is the only constant in life'. The pace of change in civilisation has accelerated in the last 50-60 years with continuous innovations in all aspects of life. With the advent of computing capabilities and continuous improvement in these capabilities along with internet-based communication, the entire landscape of the business world too has completely changed. The acceleration of the rate of change in society is only going to increase with time.

"In my view, there are two reasons for the need for 'continuous learning' for people in general and within the business world in particular," Ujjal explains. "The first is the continuous change that is happening all around us: we need to either adapt ourselves to this changing environment or be prepared to be left out of the system totally. The second is the inadequacy of our education system to prepare ourselves suitably for the world we live in. The system does not cover the basics of social skills, emotional intelligence, innovative thinking and creating an aptitude for curiosity." Learning, he stresses, is not a destination; we do not complete our education when we graduate from universities. Learning is a lifestyle.

Venkat Changavalli, Leadership Mentor, Management Consultant, Trainer and Inspirational Speaker, goes one step further. The acronym CEO, he says, also stands for Chief Educational Officer. "This encompasses learning myself and teaching others in the organisation continuously. I designed and imparted knowledge by conducting training programmes at learning forums for different levels. I also emphasised that learning can come from not just reading and training but also by observing, practising and failing."

Once you decide you want to be a student for life, several Gurus will appear. Just when you have mastered one topic something else comes up. If you have mastered strategy then execution will be next in line. If execution is mastered next could be team building.

Happy learning!

Lots of creative thinking is required to ensure that an organisation is always in the learning mode. When this happens there is enthusiasm and vibrancy in people which all translates to a successful organization.

Interview: Nishit Kumar, Founder MD, NOTRE Group

Why did you get into training, especially when you knew you would be creating competition for your own business?

My vision was to create healthy competition. I had started an advertising and public relations agency, got a couple of clients, but wasn't getting too many suitable people though I managed to hire one or two who were good. When I opened an office in Indore, I got a chance to speak at the Indore Management Association. It was then that I realised that I had to grow differently. So I convinced Symbiosis to start an evening diploma course in Advertising and PR. Many of my DAPR students joined NOTRE. And DAPR became the genesis of SIMC.

I also realised that the real issue is the culture you build in the organisation. When I was 27 years old, I announced that I would retire at the age of 45, and my number two would take over – this was not a dynasty-driven company.

How else did you make people suitable for the business?

Not only my own business, but for clients too. I took people from completely different backgrounds and retrained them. I also encouraged my colleagues to go out and take up evening courses in any related subject that would help them in their jobs, and paid the full fees for these.

This led to the setting up of NOTRE HRD – through which we provided training to a number of small and large corporations. The biggest of these was the Maharashtra State Electricity Board, for which we trained employees from linemen all the way up to the Chairman. Including major blue chip corporate and cooperatives including MNCs, they have trained over 43,000 professionals

I am also visiting faculty at a number of leading management institutes in Pune and 35 institutes in India, as also 7 countries abroad. Wherever I travel, I am also happy to address the students at various rural MBA colleges, at no charge. Now, I'm planning to set up an academic campus with a media and communications college in Pune which should start functioning from the next academic year. This will be in collaboration with a royal family and a leading media group. Another major initiative he has started is solutions for schools and colleges, especially in tier 2 and 3 cities, to enhance the business and academic performance of schools and colleges country wide.

With 2 daughters and a grandaughter, all settled in the USA, he is still raring to go.

Case Study: How a very key learning intervention can change lives?

This story is about 10 years old when I was a consultant to a company in Delhi. At that time they had a turnover of about ₹ 200 crore. The company was using a complicated manufacturing process to make some consumer durable items. In one of the most important departments, they were making casting dies in which the product would be moulded. This casting die department had a manager who had been there for the last 25 years. He had a fixed notion of working. Because of him, the company was not able to induct new talent. This guy would intimidate anybody who came in and they would leave.

At the same time the role was critical, and this manager was an expert whom the company could not get rid of. So they were living with him all this while.

One day the MD met me and told me about this problem. "What can I do?" he asked. "On one side I cannot afford to lose this guy. On the other hand I need to bring about drastic changes, otherwise I will not be able to hire new people and I will become more and more dependent as we grow. We are running a big operating risk in our business!"

So I gave him a very simple idea. It was based on the fact that people don't change because they don't see a need to change. If you are working in a company and the company recognises you and whatever you are doing is valuable to the company, then you think yours is the best and only way of doing things. So what do you do? You start believing that your methodology, your business style, your managerial style, is the best. If somebody comes and tells you, "Look, this is not the way to do things. Can you change?" You listen, but you won't do anything about it. This is the classic case.

So how do you make this man realize that he is outdated and he needs to change? We came up with the simple idea. We said we would send him for a three-month intensive training course at a middle management level to IIM Ahmedabad. At first he was not willing to go, but we convinced him. He went for the course.

When he came back after three months, the MD called me and told me that he had become an outstanding manager - more cooperative, with a changed attitude towards others.

What you do think happened to him? It's very simple. When he went to IIM Ahmedabad, he would have been benchmarked with others. First, he could not speak English. So the second day he bought a dictionary so that he could understand the language. He was talking in Hindi all this while. Most of the management concepts were completely alien to him because he could not read anything. Without being able to study, he failed miserably in the first few quizzes that IIM Ahmedabad conducted.

Then a new person emerged. Our man became totally focused on only one thing: to prove to himself and to others that he is one of the better managers. In the next three months, he slogged and struggled. But at the end of the course, he not only topped the class but also came back with the understanding that his method of working is not only the way there are thousands of other ways. This really opened his mind.

This is a very good classic story of how to break the resistance of established people, especially when they are doing well and they are very critical to the company. The bigger surprise was that when he came back he realised that the entire department had performed better in his absence. That was a big shock to him, because he had always thought that he was indispensible to the company. But the team below him had come together after he left and taken on additional responsibilities, with only one objective: to beat his record when he was away. So when this man came back, he first figured out that he was outdated and slogged to make the corrections for himself. And presto! He became a better manager.

T. Muralidharan, Chairman, TMI Group

Case Study 2: Using a learning approach, late in life, to improve your own efficiency

When I joined the corporate world in the mid-1970s, there was hardly any computing done in the business world in India. The only calculating equipment we had were expensive electronic calculators and also now-in-museum manual Facit calculators and comptometers. All the accounting and financial analysis I did was by using a team of assistants, big fat ledgers and ruled worksheets. When computers started to come into use in our organisation the mid-1980s – by which time I had become a mid-level manager – I was delegating use of computers to my assistant managers of the younger variety. Subsequently in the mid-1990s, email communication started to become popular. Again I had delegated this to my secretary, while I continued to read printouts and dictate responses. I knew I was falling behind times and I could see younger staff doing all their work themselves on their PCs.

In the year 2000, I took the call to dive in. I decided to fire my pretty secretary – of course I did it in the most pleasing way possible. I had come to the conclusion that my efficient secretary was the barrier to my learning computers. I got hold of a laptop, a mobile phone, and a voice mail on my landline. Within three or four months, I was almost at par in using computers, Word, Excel, PowerPoint etc with my younger colleagues. The learning was hard work. I had privately hired a friend's brother to coach me on basic computer skills. I made mistakes, had to type letters three times over because I forgot to save them and such silly stuff. But as time progressed, I got better and better. Some years later, it was my daughter who trained me in using Facebook and other social media.

My example forced many of my teammates at work to change their own approach to learning as well.

Ujjal Gupta, Business Coach

Case Study 3: A corollary to lifelong learning is learning about oneself

Lt. Gen. (retd) Arjun Ray,
PVSM, chief executive officer, Indus International School

Reinvention is change of identity. Physically you are the same person but you now have a new vision, a new identity as a result of your strengths or what you have achieved or not achieved. Your world view is different. There is no bitterness towards anyone. The emotions and values of love and forgiveness are paramount. you want to make a difference in the lives of others. This is the psychological profile of a reinvented individual.

Reinvention is not something deliberate. You have to wait for the right time and opportunity. It may possibly never happen. In hindsight, I feel that every person has "turning points" in life like a job, marriage, success, breakup in a relationship, debilitating illness, retirement, etc. When we arrive at any of these critical stages in our own lives, we must reflect upon what has happened or passed, learn lessons, and take new magnetic bearings.

My reinvention happened late in life, around the age of 55. There was no conscious effort or intent. It happened because of the huge success of Operation Sadbhavna in Ladakh (where I was corps commander). The socio-political campaign was successful beyond everyone's expectations. We were able to bring about peace that is still holding 16 years down the line. So the movement I started was powerful in every aspect – emotionally and spiritually. To bring about reinvention the crucible experience should be a high-voltage one. Moreover, the experience has to involve you and others. All should benefit.

The second factor is people. I believe that it is difficult to bring change within oneself without the help of other people. We are what we are because of others. When you transform other people you get transformed in the process. Transformation is, therefore, a two-way street, and the cycle continues endlessly. It is the Ladakhis who transformed me. The Africans describe this as ubantu. When you reach out, you simultaneously reach in. You may like to read up on this idea.

The third factor responsible for reinvention is the mentor. Lucky are those who have one. The mentor can guide you towards reinvention at the right time (when he or she thinks you are ready).

There is yet another factor that is seldom discussed: potential. Happiness and human motivation are derived from self-actualization; that is what we mean by potential. Man must become what he is capable of becoming. Most people never reach anywhere near what they can be. We are 'extras' in our movie of life. We are driving on a highway in first gear and constantly looking over our shoulders. No vision. No mission. And therefore, no plans. So the results are quite obvious: boredom, a feeling of resignation and despair, bitterness towards fate, melancholy, depression, etc. How to reach one's potential is a subject by itself, but in a simplistic manner it is one's ability to focus on our signature strengths. These are strengths that are unique and which other people acknowledge. It is not what you think but what others think are your signature strengths. Most are unaware. Signature strengths are your brand identity. This is what institution building is all about. Great institutions have identity! The one word in mind recall is the signature strength.

When a person is aware of his or her signature strength and makes righteous use of it, self-actualisation happens. That is when potential is reached.

Reinvention is applicable to even organisations and institutions. Changes in technology and customer psyche will necessitate reinvention. Knowledge of the market environment is absolutely essential. Critical!!

Lifelong learning is a key competency to survive and flourish in the 21st century. This is because knowledge is getting outdated rapidly. Experts estimate that by 2020 knowledge will get outdated every 24 hours. The concern for leaders and managers is that the responsibility for learning is going to be theirs. Literacy in the knowledge age is a lot about the ability for self-directed learning.

The greatest challenge is the process of re-learning, which involves unlearning and then re-learning. Unlearning is difficult because our ego and personal experiences get in the way of unbiased reflection. Unlearning can happen through cognitive dissonance and crucible experiences. Common to both these processes is the art and science of reflection. If an individual cannot reflect, experiences are meaningless. I went to wars in 1965 and 1971 but learnt nothing. Absolutely nothing. How many business leaders consciously reflect or know how to reflect?

Dissonance can be caused by a book offering contrarian views to what the reader believes in. A guru or friend or mentor can challenge your present views and provoke you to re-think. In the process she or he can get you to reflect. From a leader-perspective it is, therefore, very important to be surrounded by subordinates who are as competent if not more able than you. From the leader-perspective you must be an avid reader and listener. As a leader you will need a mentor.

Pull the plug when it does not make any sense

Don't prolong the agony to yourself or to vendors. Take it on the chin and move on. The faster, the better.

When is the right time to pull the plug? That is a million-dollar question! Is there ever a right time?

How much should one persevere? Is perseverance always good?

We started a dotcom company at the height of the dotcom boom in late 1999-early 2000. Technically the management team was a dream. There were five of us, all successful entrepreneurs, and one was an oncologist. We were setting up a health portal which was way before its time when the internet connectivity was quite pathetic — still dial-up, with little penetration. We were optimistic. I must admit we did not even have a proper business plan. We knew what we were going to do but did not have a regular revenue stream. It was all a bit vague.

However, we foolishly spent money – our own and also money from some investors who happened to be family and friends. One of the first lessons here is, never borrow from family and friends - you are obliged to pay back everything if the business goes bust. With private equity or angel investment you have the luxury of a business going belly-up and not having to dip into your children's or family's funds to pay off the debtors.

So we ran the business for almost a year. At the end of the year we had some investors interested, but their stipulations for putting in the money were not agreeable to us. We put in some more of our hard-earned money, travelled, met people, put in content, built the portal twice over which cost us a bomb. Basically, we did everything possible which we should not have done. In one year's time, when we still could not think of a sustainable revenue stream, we decided to pull the plug. Also, the management team started disbanding one by one and only two of us were left holding the can. So we lost money — a fairly big sum – but we wound up the business before throwing more good money after bad.

Ironically, the business was called Good Morning Doctor. That became 'good night' quickly.

Lessons learnt:

- What is the revenue stream?

- Who will be the customer?

- Why should the customer buy from me?

- How many times will he buy from me?

- Do I have a competitive edge?

- Is the business sustainable?

- Is it scalable?

- Why am I in it in the first place?

- Do I have any moat around to protect my idea, or is it easily replicated?

Most importantly

- How much money do I have to sustain the business if it is too premature?

- How am I going to fund it? From debt and/or equity?

- How will I pay back? Will I be generating enough revenue to pay my interest + instalments?

- When will the breakeven be?

- How much more money do I need?

Finally, it is about finance again. Back to Chapter 4 and Dr Anil Lamba! Despite having a very good product or service, planning for finance plays a key role.

We do keep going back and forth: here, the Business India television disaster comes back to mind. Ashok Advani obviously didn't see all these signals, but kept going on sheer optimism alone. BiTV was a good idea, but very obviously too much before its time – and Ashok could not generate the revenue to pay back his debts.

From my practical experience I can say the good time to pull the plug is when you do not see any light at the end of the tunnel. When finances totally dry up. Period. When there is no money to be made in the venture. When you missed paying the staff for a year on time. When you know deep down that the honourable thing to do is pull the plug. Better to take it on the chin and move on.

There are times I have done this for a bad stock investment or bad client. Yes, people who have a lot of persistence think that any situation is salvageable; but the question which needs to be asked is: is it worth salvaging and what exactly are you holding up? Your ego or the business? Clarity between the two will probably help make the decision in a cool, calm and rational frame of mind. Anyway the rule of the corporate jungle is such that if you don't pull the plug it is going to happen anyway. So it is better you do it so it can be done in an organized fashion rather than being forced to do it unceremoniously, with all your goodwill having evaporated and yielded place to badwill instead. Many businesses have perhaps kept it for when it is too late and there is nothing left. So then Mr Market pulls the plug for you.

Loss of enthusiasm is another very good reason to pull the plug on a business. If you do not have that fire in your belly to get up in the morning and go change the world, then your interest in the business has dipped. When you find this happening persistently, you may decide to merge, sell your stake and get out.

Also, what if your product has no takers? Your gut instinct may have said there is plenty of potential in the marketplace; but in actuality there is no market for it. It happens in software, e-commerce, hardware, some types of services, kitchen appliances. Many times a product is simply too premature. I would say our health portal still has no takers and there is no revenue model for the same 12 years after we pulled the plug. No regrets at all.

Back again, to Chapter 2: Achal Bakeri found no takers for his extended range of products that would take his brand beyond just the seasonal summertime air coolers. His money dried up. So he did the smart thing, and re-tuned his Symphony around the good music that his primary product provided.

Of course, it can so happen that there may be light at the end of the tunnel just about the time when you pulled the plug. There are some possibilities an entrepreneur can consider before pulling the plug. Here's a list of what you can consider.

Alliances? Somebody may be interested in clubbing their revenue model with yours, thereby making it a complete offering.

Another highly profitable company may want to take on a loss-making one if they feel it has potential to turn it around and finance is the only stumbling block.

Your product may have takers in another country albeit in a different format.

You may have content which can be syndicated perhaps?

If you are in manufacturing, a larger company may want to take over your business because you have some unique customers to whom they can pitch their other existing products.

Net net: evaluate all the possibilities and if you feel as if there is no hope at all then the wisest - and kindest - thing would be to pull the plug.

From our own example why we did just that:

1. The key promoters were all in different businesses and nobody was really dedicated to the portal.

2. There was no revenue model in sight.

3. Dotcom as an industry was slowly going bust - all with similar business models of no revenue but sexy businesses.

4. Finance had dried up.

5. We realized that much more good money had to be funnelled in and still there was no revenue in sight.

6. The promoters had lost their enthusiasm.

7. Finally, the reasons we got into the business also might have been wrong.

Go back again, and refer to Chapter 1 if you have missed the reasons why you should be in business!

The only good thing was that we did not have too many employees and we could pay all our vendors, employees, rents and money to various investors. However if business is not run like a business but more for an ego massage, then one is unlikely to pull the plug at all. We have seen promoters going down or being forcibly evicted by the bank.

In all fairness, it is difficult to pull the plug in India. The social stigma is too high. Also, our society and cultural milieu are such that risk-taking is not encouraged, nor are there enough angel investors. As of 2014-15 the scenario has changed. Angel investors are lining up to get a piece of the action in India. The bankruptcy law itself is very weak.

Bankruptcy is a legally declared inability or impairment of ability of an individual or organization to pay its creditors. Creditors may file a bankruptcy petition against a business or corporate debtor ("involuntary bankruptcy") in an effort to recoup a portion of what they are owed or initiate a restructuring. In the majority of cases, however, bankruptcy is initiated by the debtor (a "voluntary bankruptcy" that is filed by the insolvent individual or organization). An involuntary bankruptcy petition may not be filed against an individual consumer debtor who is not engaged in business.

Bankruptcy was originally planned as a remedy for creditors — not debtors. During the reign of King Henry VIII, bankruptcy law allowed a creditor to seize all of the assets of a trader who could not pay his debts. Additionally, on top of losing all of one's property, the unfortunate debtor also lost his freedom and was subject to imprisonment for failure to pay his debts. This left the family of the debtor in the position of having to pay the debts in order to obtain the release of the debtor.

India does not have a clear law on corporate bankruptcy even though individual bankruptcy laws have been in existence since 1874. The current law in force was enacted in 1920 called Provincial Insolvency Act which consists of Chapter 7 and Chapter 13 bankruptcies.

The legal meaning of the terms bankruptcy, insolvency, liquidation and dissolution are contested in the Indian legal system. There is no regulation or statute legislated upon bankruptcy which denotes a condition of inability to meet a demand of a creditor as is common in many other jurisdictions.

Winding up of companies is in the jurisdiction of the Courts which can take a decade even after the Company has actually been declared insolvent. On the other hand, supervisory restructuring at the behest of The Board of Industrial and Financial Reconstruction is generally undertaken using receivership by a Public Finance Institution.

India has bankruptcy laws dating as old as 1874… and today's law clearly demarcates the business/company's assets from the personal assets… it distinguishes between the assets of the family and your assets, and has all the features that allow you to write-off the loan once and for all and start again. (*SOURCE: Lexvidhi*)

In developed countries, notably the U.S, declaring bankruptcy is normal and the entrepreneur can go on to other businesses fairly successfully. Under Chapter 16, one can virtually walk in through one door, file forms for bankruptcy and walk out through the other door to set up another company. Such instances are few in India. So if one sees it from the Indian perspective it is quite understandable why a businessman would be most reluctant to pull the plug but consider it as a last resort, rarely doing it proactively.

Back again to Achal Bakeri whom you met in Chapter 2. The son of a successful civil engineer who got into real estate development, he decided to venture out on his own after studying architecture and did a US MBA. Achal, then 28, was thrilled when his Symphony air coolers became a success — all his family and friends whom he called to see it liked the product, and the subsequent response from the market was 'phenomenal'. But when he spread his wings into products that were not restricted to one season, summer, they all bombed! Symphony went bust. Luckily, he saw sense: he reworked his strategy, exited everything else and concentrated again on air coolers. From 2002 onwards, Symphony became a single-product company again – and in six years it was healthy again. Achal and Symphony are the kings of the air-cooler market again – and the turning point was his timely decision to pull the plug.

But by the time Ashok H. Advani finally decided to pull the plug on his ill-fated television venture, the company had been kept bleeding for too long. He owed crores – including salaries and other dues to the employees of the company he finally shut down, as well as the parent company he still runs. He still does.

Which was better?

Interview: T. Muralidharan, Founder & Chairman, TMI Group

You are running what is obviously a successful human resources consulting and training firm. Where did you have to pull the plug?

I wasn't always in Human Resources and training. I graduated from IIT Madras in 1979 and did my MBA from IIM Ahmedabad. Then I teamed up with a friend who was also at IIM-A, and we set up a seeds business. He was an agriculture graduate. We put together all our savings and borrowings, to talling ₹ 25,000. We made a very rational decision: that we would try to make a go of it, but if it didn't take off by the time we spent that money, we would get out. We knew that Hyderabad has always been India's seeds capital, so it was the obvious choice. We moved here and started. The business flopped, and we stuck to our original plan of winding it up.

Wasn't that enough experience to put you off enterprise forever?

No. I was still determined to make it in business. To be honest, things got very bleak in 1991, 10 years after I got my MBA and got out into the wide world. But an accidental encounter put me on another path. My wife is a journalist. One of her friends dropped in at home and used my telephone to make calls for her own head-hunting business. I said to myself, why shouldn't I get into recruitment too? So I did. I set up TMI Inputs & Services Pvt. Ltd the same year.

Were all these ventures great successes?

Again, no. I lost money at the rate of ₹ 50 lakh a month in my first new venture, too. I had no revenues. My losses mounted, till they hit ₹ 4 crore in 2004. But I persevered. I learned more from my failures than my later success. Mainly, that funding is very important, though we tend to underestimate its value. Nine years after TMI Inputs & Services, I established my second company, C&K (content and knowledge) Management Ltd, with venture-capital funding on a US$6-million valuation by ICICI Ventures; and in 2011 I set up the third, TMI e2E (education to employment) Academy.

And?

My TMI group has 1,000-plus employees today. We have a pan-India presence. We have provided recruitment, training and technology services in the HR space for over 3,000 leading companies. We do everything from single hires to 3,000 at a shot, across professions from ITI diploma holders to chartered accountants. We also do everything in talent acquisition, end to end: TMI works with NSDC (National Skills Development Council) for graduate employability, do entry-level campus recruitment at monthly salaries of ₹ 7,000 and hire mid-level to senior management executives for up to ₹ 10 lakh. We also provide on-the-job skill development. In a nutshell, we cater to the employability and training needs of professionals through their entire lifecycle in an organisation. The group has recruited more than 50,000 people in the two decades of its existence, about 15,000 of whom I have interviewed myself. I continue to be a hands-on Chairman!

Case Study: No lobsters in the pot!

When Inayat Shukur decided to move from the hectic pace of life in Bombay to the laid-back coastal town of Murud after he quit corporate life at age 60, he decided to farm lobsters. "We had a house on a hill overlooking the sea, and lots of friends and relatives used to drop in for weekends or other breaks," he says. One day, a visiting cousin from Madras, who had lobster pots off the eastern coast, suggested that they team up do the same thing together on the west. The cousin had all the overseas contacts, and tied up everything for exports to Hong Kong, intended for the Chinese mainland. Inayat organised the Murud-Bombay side of things: catching the crustaceans, carting them to the airport and the right flights to get them to the buyer in time, fresh. Every day, Inayat would walk down to the beach, check the haul, follow the shipment in a six-seater auto-rickshaw, take a launch across the bay and a taxi to the airport, to ensure that everything went off without a hitch. Things picked up, and he was soon exporting 1.5 tonnes a month.

But the cost of the operation –the expenses in harvesting the lobsters, the fees of the fishermen who checked and brought in the lobster pots, and freight rates - went up, and the buyers were not interested in paying so much. Overfishing by the locals even during the monsoon, when the activity is officially banned and boats are not supposed to go out, also reduced the spawning drastically, and soon there were very few lobsters in the pots.

"So I decided after a year and a half that enough was enough. I too went back home to Bombay, returning to my Murud home only for occasional breaks – sometimes alone, often with my mother and sister or friends. No more lobsters!" he says. But would he go back to the business today? "No," he says. "The problem is still the same - worse, in fact. There are fewer lobsters out there, and the cost of catching, trucking and airlifting them is prohibitive."

Epilogue

At the outset, I want to thank some of the people who made this book possible. At the top of the list is my dear friend Nishit Kumar, who gave me frank details of all his troubles and mistakes in business so that others won't make them too. Nishit – public relations professional par excellence and 'Sir' to so many young people whom he helped build their own careers – was not too happy with how I portrayed the negatives in his entrepreneurial endeavors, but that didn't stop him from pushing people at all levels in academia and elsewhere to order copies. He died on 26 December 2014, leaving a gaping void in the lives of so many of us: family, friends, shagirds…

My thanks also to those who took the trouble to go through the book and provide detailed inputs which will help us replicate and exceed the runaway success of the first print run. First off the mark was Ujjal Gupta, my school friend from the 1968 Higher Secondary batch of St. Lawrence High School, Calcutta. Ujjal – whom I have quoted at length a number of times in the book – read the whole thing word by word and e-mailed two lists: of 'Suggestions for possible improvements in presentation', and 'Typos and other proofing errors noticed'. Needless to say, we've incorporated all of those in this second imprint.

Fr Guy Kenneth Carlson, sj, who taught us at good old St. Lawrence and now lives in Australia, took just as much as trouble at age 86 and sent me a long list of mistakes we had made. And though he doesn't know Kiran Bhat, he gladdened her heart with his appreciation of the book being 'inspirational in some quite spiritual ways': with its many passages about helping others, enthusing them, advancing them and improving things for the country. He even says he could make use of these for sermons in church and keep people spellbound with our stories and examples!

Some of my family and friends, who previewed this book, had one question: if it's co-authored, why does it say 'I' so often ? The answer is simple: this is basically Kiran's book- about her experiences as an entrepreneur, which she wants to pass on so that newbies in the field can learn some lessons. Being an old friend, she called me in to help with case studies, interviews and examples of other entrepreneurs I have met and written about. So obviously, her accounts are first person and my inputs are third person.

When we got into this project in October 2013, we had discussed nine principles of entrepreneurship. I've covered entrepreneurs of all kinds during my 23-plus years in Business India, and loved the idea. As a journalist, especially a business journalist, I've always believed that the 'interest' factor so necessary to any story is of far more value than the 'importance' factor. If something – an event, a person, a company – is important, it will get covered anyway - even if the man on the spot doesn't, someone from headquarters is sure to.

That's what makes entrepreneurship so fascinating: the small guy (or girl), struggling against odds – mainly family, and then finance – and struggling to make it on his or her own. This is the stuff stories are made of, the newly-married young man pawning his wife's jewellery to start an industrial unit he has long dreamt of, the young woman flying in the face of tradition and blazing a new trail in online marketing or service apartments. Obviously, not all of them succeed. Some go on to build empires, list their companies on the stock exchanges, and become rich – though that, as we have pointed out in the book, is the worst possible reason to get into entrepreneurship. Many flounder and finally fail, to listen to the "I told you so!" that family and friends are so prompt to say.

But it is their trials and travails on their chosen trail that grips the imagination. The successes never have it all easy, even those born with silver spoons in their mouths and the contacts and resources to make their roads less thorny. Those who start out without any advantages but the burning desire to "do something" – new and different, building a better mousetrap – have to travel on buses, pound the streets and barge into potential customers' offices on the strength of a necktie, a jacket and an air of supreme confidence when they are cringing inside.

And therein lies a tale: the tale we have tried to tell in this book, that there are no, repeat no, holy cows.

But nobody in our family has ever done business! You should also get a good job and settle down!

You are a girl from a respectable family. You can't go to meet strange people and sell them products and services. Anyway, it's high time you got married.

Where do you think you are going to get the money from? All I have is kept separate for your sister's wedding.

All our relatives, friends and neighbours will laugh at us. How will we get your sister married?

If you are the kind of person who wants to think out of the box, go against the traditional 'wisdom' of settling down in a safe job or a safe marriage, these principles - and stories - are for you. We hope we have managed to achieve at least part of what we set out do: get young people, who are at the threshold of a career, thinking about alternatives.

If you have fire in your belly, don't dowse it – stoke it, and see where it takes you.

Sekhar Seshan

About the Authors

KIRAN BHAT

Kiran is a first generation entrepreneur. She started Xebec Communications Pvt ltd an advertising agency offering integrated communications in 1992. She has handled blue chip clients in various sectors ranging from automobiles, BFSI, Retail, Real estate, Services etc. In her role as strategist and brand consultant she has launched several brands in India. Anticipating the advent of digital she promoted a second company Xebec digital with a pan India presence which offers digital consultancy, creative technology and marketing. Right from the early stages of her career she has been teaching in management institutes and is often invited as guest lecturer. She has several other interests. She has been an angel investor in several start ups and likes nothing more than mentoring starts ups to do better than what she has done. Her other interests include fine art, writing, alternate healing. She likes to read new age spiritual and management thought leaders.

Kiran is a post graduate in Industrial Psychology from the University of Pune. She has done Executive Education "Aligning Strategy with Execution" from HBS and been a rank holder at graduate level. Has won several awards for entrepreneurship from the Rotary and several educational institutes. She lives in Pune with her husband and daughter but considers herself a global citizen.

SEKHAR SESHAN

Sekhar has been a journalist since 1972, after earning a post-graduate (B.Sc, chemistry!) degree in journalism, B.J. He began with a local Pune newspaper, Poona Herald (now Sakal Times), moved on to children's magazine Sunshine and then wire service United News of India (UNI) in Bombay, which he left after 12 years as Chief Sub-editor in charge of Maharashtra, Gujarat and Goa. After a four-year hiccup in public relations (with Ogilvy & Mather), he was in Business India from July 1989 till his retirement in October 2012. He continues to dabble in magazine journalism, as Consultant Editor with Business India and Corporate Tycoons, Member of the Editorial Board of Business for All and a contributor to Corporate Citizen. He is also Editor of SNAP BOOKS, a four-man army of veterans in photography, design, writing and marketing that takes complete contracts for business biographies.

He lives in Pune with wife Dr Radhika Seshan, associate professor in History at University of Pune, and daughters Nisha, who teaches at the Alliance Francaise and is a Bharatanatyam exponent and teacher, and Varsha, who writes children's fiction, conducts writing and dance workshops and is also a Bharatanatyam exponent and teacher.

For updates and **No Holy Cows** wisdom follow us:
No Holy Cows in Business, @noholycows, www.noholycows.com

Appendix
Acronyms

Many of these may be familiar to Indian readers, but they are expanded for those abroad; many of the corporations have been formally renamed by the initials, so the full names are only a matter of record.

CMD: Chairman & Managing Director

LPG: Liquefied Petroleum Gas

TDS: Tax Deducted at Source

R&D: Research and Development

IT: Information Technology

CA: Chartered Accountant/Accountancy

DCM: The erstwhile Delhi Cloth Mills

IDBI: Industrial Development Bank of India

ICICI: Industrial Credit and Investment Corporation of India

IFCI: Industrial Finance Corporation of India

PC: Personal Computer

USP: Unique Selling Proposition

TCS: Tata Consultancy Services

MAA: Marketing & Advertising Associates

CFO: Chief Financial Officer

LIC: Life Insurance Corporation of India

PBT: Profit Before Tax

GAAP: Generally Accepted Accounting Principles

Q1: Quarter One (First Quarter of Financial Year)

IVRCL: Iragavarapu Venkata Reddy Construction Limited

HDO: Hindustan Dorr-Oliver

CEO: Chief Executive Officer

EMRI: Emergency Management & Research Institute

FD: Fixed Deposit

SEO: Search Engine Optimization

SEM: Search Engine Marketing

HMV: His Master's Voice, The Gramophone Company of India

MBA: Master in Business Administration

IIM: Indian Institute of Management

ITI: Industrial Training Institute

Index

Aachi Masala, A.D. Padmasingh Isaac, 4

Ambuja Neotia Group, Harshvardhan Neotia, 12

Aziz Poonawalla, 52

Backpackers, Rajesh Shaw, 10

Bharat Nain, 52

Business India, Ashok H. Advani, 62, 145, 150

Calvin Klein, 82

Country Club India, Y. Rajeev Reddy, 5, 23

Dass Electric, Naresh Sareen, 65, 99

Demag, Suhas Baxi, 81, 121

DRS Group/Agarwal Packers & Movers, Dayanand Agarwal, 112

Granules India/KRSMA Wines, Uma Chigurupati & C. Kishna Prasad, 14

GVK Group, G.V. Krishna Reddy, 103

Harish Bijoor, 22, 102

Inayat Shukur, 152s

Indian Map Service, Dr R.P. Arya, 41

Indus International School, Lt. Gen (retd) Arjun Ray, 139

Infosys, Narayanamurthy, 130

i-Vista, Narayan Rajan, 66, 100

IVRCL, E. Sudhir Reddy, 107

Karvy Group, C. Parthasarathy, 47

Lakme, 82

Lamcon School of Management, Anil Lamba, 69, 145

MH Group, Siddharth Patel, 112, 113

Nath Biogene, Satish Kgliwal, 89

NOTRE, Nishit Kumar, 98, 135

Nuziveedu Seeds, M. Prabhakar Rao, 88

Partha system, 56

Pench Tiger Resort, Sandeep Singh, 9

Punjab Tractors, Chandra Mohan, 27

Rico Auto Industries, Arvind Kapur, 79, 80

RSB Group, R.K. Behera, 50

Sakra World Hospital, Geetanjali Kirloskar, 96

Sandhar Technologies, Jayant Davar, 6, 79, 80

Siddha Samadhi Yoga, Sanjay Thakker, 18, 119

Sleep-Ins, Kishor Chhabria, 64

Srei, Hemant Kanoria, 72

Strand Book Stall, T.N. Shanbhag, 30

Sulajja Firodia Motwani, 2

Sun Pharmaceutical Industries, Dilip Shanghvi, 86

Symphony, Achal Bakeri, 5, 24, 146, 149

TalentSprint, Santanu Paul, 115, 132

TMI Group, T. Muralidharan, 138, 150

Toyota Kirloskar Motor, Vikram S. Kirloskar, 84

Ujjal Gupta, Business Coach, 116, 122, 133, 138/9

Vadilal Industries, Rajesh Gandhi, 42

Venkat Changavalli, Leadership Mentor, 115, 134